ORIGAMI
Bugs & Beasts

Manuel Sirgo Álvarez

DOVER PUBLICATIONS, INC.
Mineola, New York

**I dedicate this book to
Olivia and Manuel, my parents**

Bibliographical Note

This Dover edition, first published in 2007, is a new English translation of all the text from *Papiroinsectos y otros origamis exóticos,* originally published in Spanish by Editorial Miguel A. Salvatella, S.A., Barcelona, Spain, in 2004, and includes all of the original diagrams and illustrations.

Library of Congress Cataloging-in-Publication Data

Sirgo Álvarez, Manuel, 1960–
  [Papiroinsectos y otros origamis exóticos. English]
  Origami bugs and beasts / Manuel Sirgo Álvarez.
    p. cm.
  ISBN-13: 978-0-486-46192-2
  ISBN-10: 0-486-46192-0
    1. Origami. 2. Insects in art. I. Title.

TT870.S524 2007
736'.982—dc22

                                                         2007026701

Manufactured in the United States of America
Dover Publications, Inc., 31 East 2nd Street, Mineola, N.Y. 11501

ORIGAMI
Bugs & Beasts

Prologue

I first met Manuel Sirgo in 2000, when I was in charge of the Spanish Origami Association's (AEP — *Asociación Española de Papiroflexia*) virtual store, where he was a frequent customer. At first, the only thing that I knew about him was that he bought practically everything that had ever been published on origami. I soon found out that besides being a compulsive "paper folder," he was also the creator of a large collection of models, most of them of insects. The first models I saw were surprisingly good for someone who had been practicing origami for less than a year. They were quite promising, although their potential had not been fully developed.

Throughout 2001, I was able to observe the constant evolution of his technique. Even though all of his models started with traditional bases, he achieved incredible results with them.

By May of 2002, when I met Manuel in person at the National AEP Convention, he had already diagrammed over 80 models. Their level of difficulty ranged from "not too difficult" to "absolutely impossible."

What can I tell you about Manuel? He is neither short nor tall, neither fat nor thin, but he has something that is not easy to find among people interested in origami: he understands paper. His folding process constantly tests the paper's resistance, but does not tear it. He is able to stretch internal layers in ways that seem impossible. The most surprising thing of all is that when you fold the paper according to his instructions, it does not turn out to be that difficult at all. You get pointed angles out of thin air, and figures so real that they seem to be alive. Another of his outstanding features is that he works really hard, and when he puts his mind to something, he always delivers; and yet, he still manages to find enough time to fold impossible figures.

J. Aníbal Voyer

ontents

Part 1. MARINE INVERTEBRATES

6

Part 2. MAMMALS

Part 3. INSECTS

Part 4. ARACHNIDS

7

Part 5. OTHER EXOTIC CREATURES

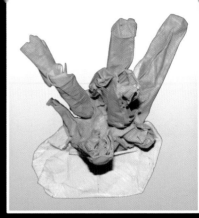

Sponge
p. 25

Sea Urchin
p. 28

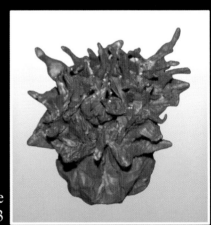

Anemone
p. 33

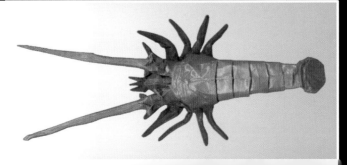

Lobster
p. 38

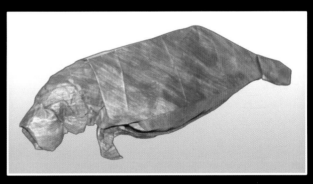

Sea Lion   p. 44

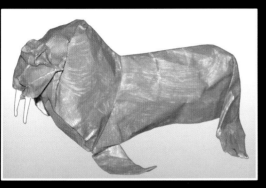

Walrus   p. 48

9

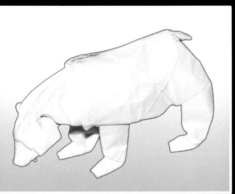

Manatee   p. 51

Polar Bear   p. 54

Harlequin Beetle (Male)
p. 66

Timberman Beetle
p. 60

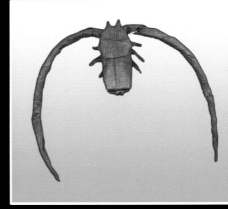

Centipede
p. 58

pine Longhorn Beetle
p. 87

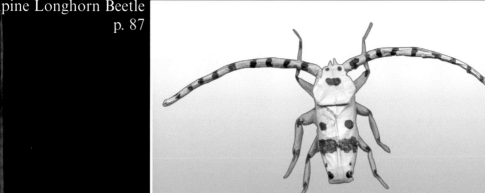

Stag Beetle
p. 77

Goliath Beetle   p. 81

11

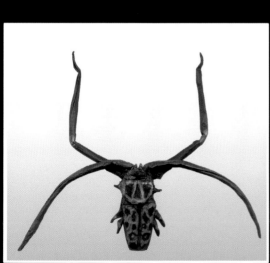

Harlequin Beetle (Female)
p. 71

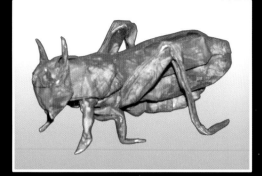

Migratory Locust
p. 94

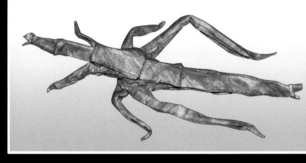

Stick Grasshopper
p. 99

12

Giant Australian Earwig
p. 103

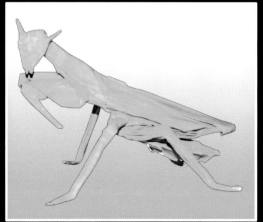

Praying Mantis
p. 111

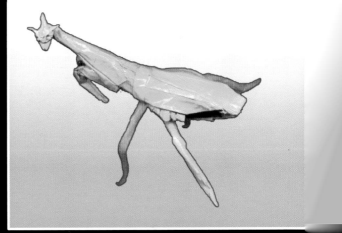

Tarantula   p. 145

Orb-weaver Spider   p. 13[8]

Red-legged Spider
p. 141

Scorpion
p. 154

European Tree Frog   p. 162

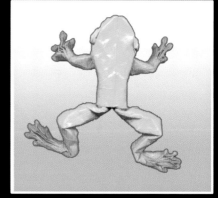

Centaurea
p. 169

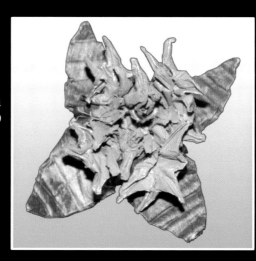

15

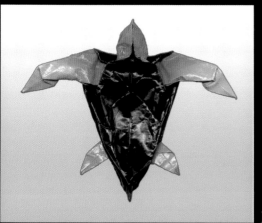

Leatherback Sea Turtle   p. 172

Preface

My name is Manuel Sirgo and I was born in Valladolid, Spain. I have lived in León, France, for more than 15 years. I teach physics, chemistry, and math to high school students. I have been a member of the Spanish Origami Association (AEP—*Asociación Española de Papiroflexia*) since 2001 and I am currently the coordinator for their newsletter's editorial group.

I've been interested in origami since I was a child. The first figure I learned to fold was an airplane. My father taught me how to do it when I was six years old. After that, I started to learn the classic figures every kid learns in school in Spain: little birds, boats, etc. When I was twelve, I bought a book called *El mundo de papel (The World of Paper),* written by Dr. Montero, who coincidentally had been my pediatrician when I was a child. By the time I learned how to make all the figures in that book, origami had become a fun hobby.

Over many years, I folded those figures countless times (especially the Japanese Frog and the Flower). Then, I started to fold the figures in *Papirogami,* written by Vicente Palacios. In the mid-90s, I found a book called *El libro de las pajaritas de papel (The Book of Folded Paper Birds),* published by the Riglos group. It had some spectacular figures that made me start to think of origami as something other than just a pastime; I started to appreciate its artistic aspects, too.

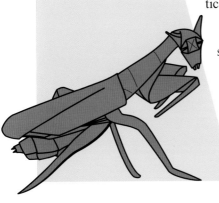

My current immersion into the world of origami started in the summer of 2000, when I bought two books: *Seres de Ficción (Fictional Beings),* by Mario Adrados and Aníbal Voyer, and *Papiroflexia para Expertos (Origami for Experts),* by Kasahara. When I read those books, I started to realize that origami is not an accidental process of folding paper; instead, it is an enthusiastic planning process, which can go well, or not, in order to achieve what one wants.

In only two years, my origami library grew from six to sixty books. I bought books by Montroll, Lang, Brill, Albertino, Kawahata, Gilgado, Halle, etc. I will not list them all here, as I do not wish to bore you, but I am sure that I have forgotten to mention at least one of them.

The first figure I invented was the orb-weaver spider, of which I am quite fond. Most of my figures start out with traditional bases. I am now taking the first steps in designing specific bases, which are adapted to each figure using mathematical methods.

I like models that demand a medium to high level of difficulty. For the most complex models in this book, such as the arthropods, I recommend that you use thin, metallic, or "sandwich" paper. I usually paint the white side of metallic papers with water-based paint (watercolors), depending on the model. "Sandwich" paper is made by gluing together a layer of silk paper, a layer of aluminum foil and then another layer of silk paper. The best glues for this process are glue sticks and spray glues, such as those used in photography.

I would like to thank the many people, such as Ronald Koh and Aníbal Voyer, who encouraged me to publish these figures when they saw the photos of them. I would also like to thank my wife (Nelly) and my children (Marta and Víctor, who are three and five years old) for the time that I have not spent with them while I was drawing these models. I would also like to thank my parents, siblings, nieces, and nephews for their encouragement and remarks. I would like to thank Aníbal Voyer, Mario Adrados, and Fernando Gilgado for their great computer generated drawings based on the drafts I showed them. I also appreciate the help of Alfredo Pérez, Pere Olivella, Francisco Ramón Navarro, and Carlos González Santamaría (who offered suggestions and encouragement during the first folding process of the book's figures), as well as the help of the aforementioned drafters. I would also like to specifically thank Nicolas Terry for the magnificent and selfless distribution of my models through his website: http://design.origami.free.fr and his contribution to the folding process of some models.

I hope that your figures turn out well.

Kind regards,
Manuel Sirgo

17

SYMBOLS

For experienced paper folders, origami symbols are a rich and powerful language, so they do not need any additional explanations. Fortunately for beginners, the meaning of the majority of symbols is so obvious that no additional comments are needed.

In this section, you will find explanations for the basic symbols used throughout the book. We suggest that you spend a few minutes studying them before you start to fold your figures.

Valley Fold

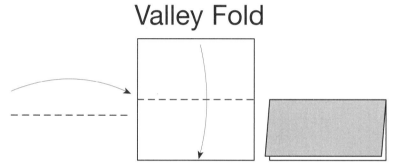

A Valley Fold is indicated by a dashed line and an arrow with a symmetric head that shows how the paper will be folded. In this example, the paper is folded in the middle and the top side joins the bottom side.

Mountain Fold

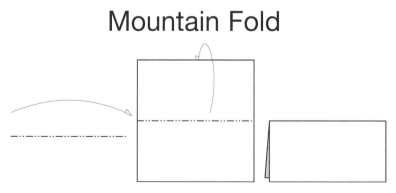

A Mountain Fold has a dashed and dotted line and an arrow with an asymmetric head that shows how the paper will be folded. In general, when these types of arrows are shown, the paper should be folded away from you, which is the opposite of a Valley Fold.

Fold and Unfold

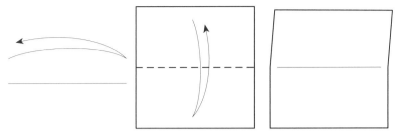

Fold the paper the same way as a Valley Fold. After folding it, unfold it to its original position. The only thing that will change is that there will now be a crease on the paper.

Layered Fold

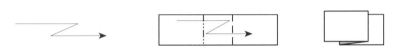

This fold consists of a Valley Fold and a Mountain Fold. The arrow, as usual, will show the movement of the folding and give us an idea of the final result, shown sideways.

Accordian Fold

This process includes two or more consecutive folds on the same side. They can be Valley or Mountain Folds, since the process is the same.

Sink Fold

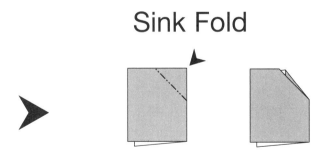

Press in the corner until it is folded under the upper layer. The model should still be flat after this is done.

Rotate

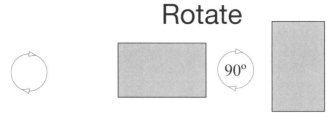

Rotate the model in the direction shown by the arrows in the symbol. The rotation angle is written inside the symbol.

Turn Over

The symbol is made up of an arrow with a loop, which indicates that we should turn the paper over, putting the side that was facing up, down on the table.

Enlarged View

This means that the next step of the diagram is drawn on a larger scale, so that it can be more easily understood.

Reduced View

This arrow is usually used after an enlarged figure has been shown, after the folds have been completed, and we have gone back to the smaller scale view.

Repeat

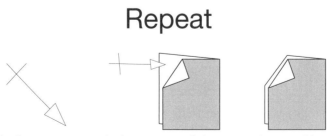

This symbol asks us to repeat the last steps and shows us where and how many times they should be repeated (depending on the number of lines the arrow has).

1

part

21

Jellyfish

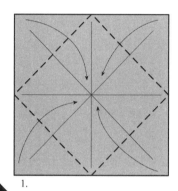

1.

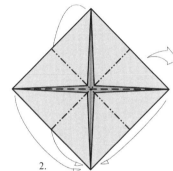

2.

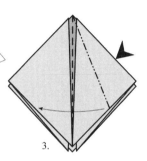

3.

4.

5.

6.

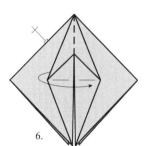

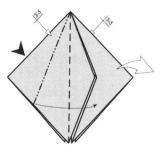

7. Repeat steps 3 to 5 on
the front and reverse sides.

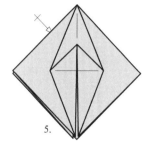

8.

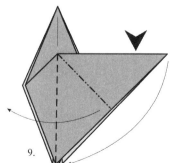

9.

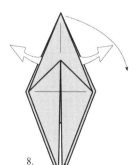

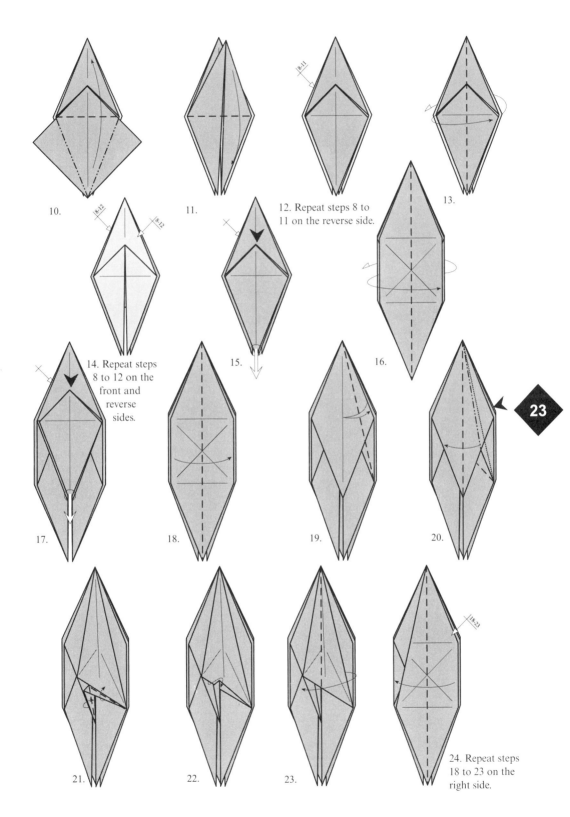

10.

11.

12. Repeat steps 8 to 11 on the reverse side.

13.

14. Repeat steps 8 to 12 on the front and reverse sides.

15.

16.

23

17.

18.

19.

20.

21.

22.

23.

24. Repeat steps 18 to 23 on the right side.

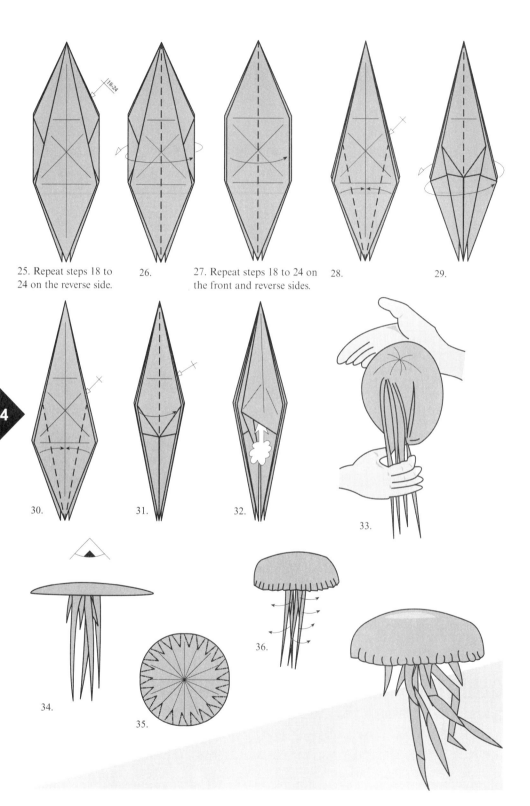

25. Repeat steps 18 to 24 on the reverse side.

26.

27. Repeat steps 18 to 24 on the front and reverse sides.

28.

29.

24

30.

31.

32.

33.

34.

35.

36.

Sponge

1.

2.

3.

4.

5.

6.

7.

8.

9. Repeat steps 6 to 9.

10.

11.

12.

13.

14.

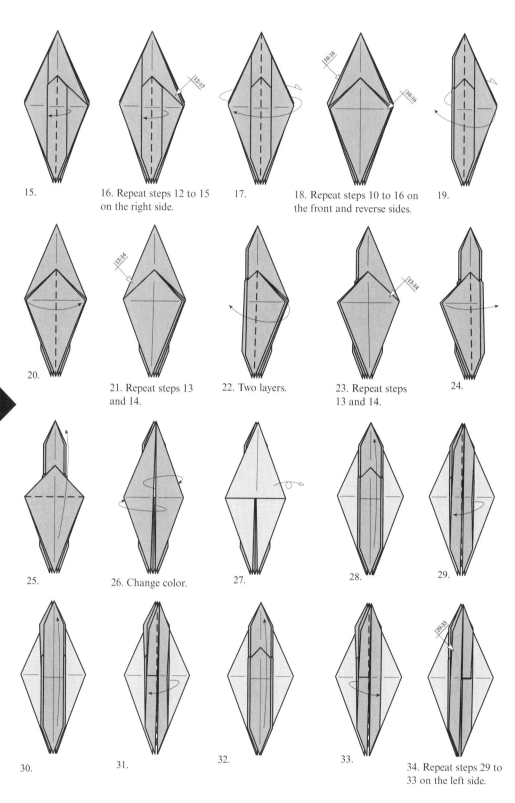

15.

16. Repeat steps 12 to 15 on the right side.

17.

18. Repeat steps 10 to 16 on the front and reverse sides.

19.

20.

21. Repeat steps 13 and 14.

22. Two layers.

23. Repeat steps 13 and 14.

24.

25.

26. Change color.

27.

28.

29.

30.

31.

32.

33.

34. Repeat steps 29 to 33 on the left side.

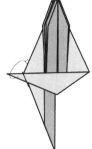

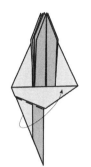

38.

39. Take hold of all the tips and place them in a vertical position.

35.

36. Stick the tip into the reverse side pocket.

37.

Tubes

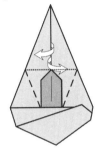

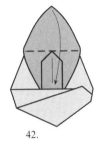

43. Fold at the base of the tubes.

42.

40. Tubes are not shown on the following steps.

41.

HOW TUBES ARE FOLDED

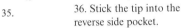

27

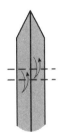

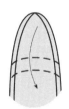

44. Long tubes.

45. Separate.

46. Sink the tube and shape it into a cylinder to form the osculum.

47. Repeat the process for the rest of the tubes, but give them different lengths.

48. Short tubes.

49. Sink the tubes and shape it into a cylinder to form the osculum.

50.

51. The middle tip is similar to smaller tubes.

Sea Urchin

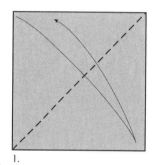

1.

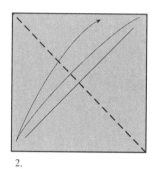

2.

3.

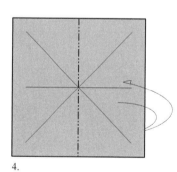

4.

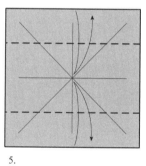

5.

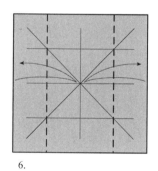

6.

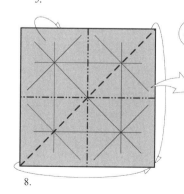

7.

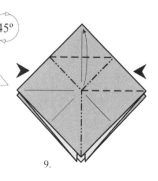

8.

45°

9.

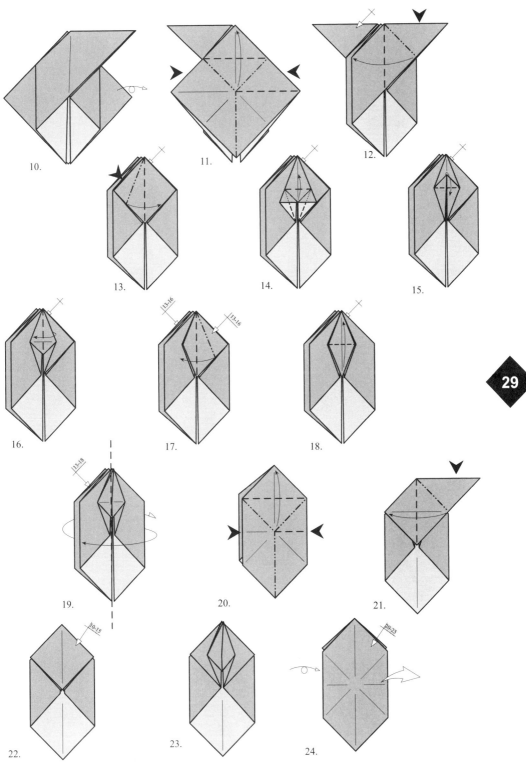

10.

11.

12.

13.

14.

15.

16.

17.

18.

19.

20.

21.

22.

23.

24.

29

25.

26.

27.

28.

29.

30

30.

31. 25-31 · 25-31

32.

33. 33

34. 33 · 33

35. Closed
sink fold.

36.

37.

38.

39.

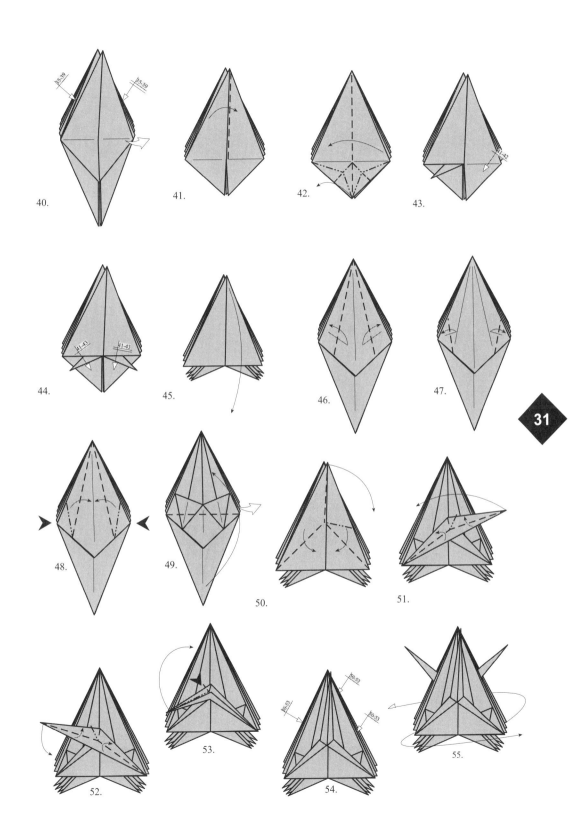

40.

41.

42.

43.

44.

45.

46.

47.

31

48.

49.

50.

51.

52.

53.

54.

55.

56.

57.

58.

59.

60.

61.

62.

63.

64.

65. Unfasten.

66.

67. Double rabbit ear.

68.

69.

70. Flatten the tip to make it thinner.
Shape it so that it becomes rounder.

Anemone

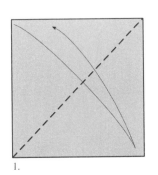

1.

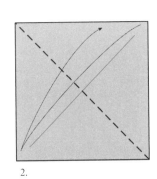

2.

3.

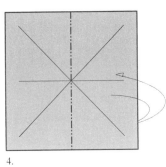

4.

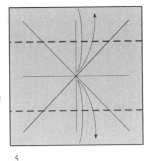

5.

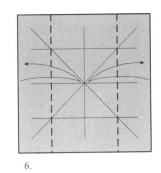

6.

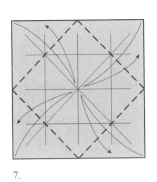

7.

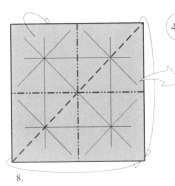

8.

45°

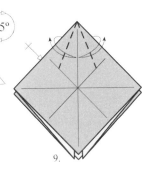

9.

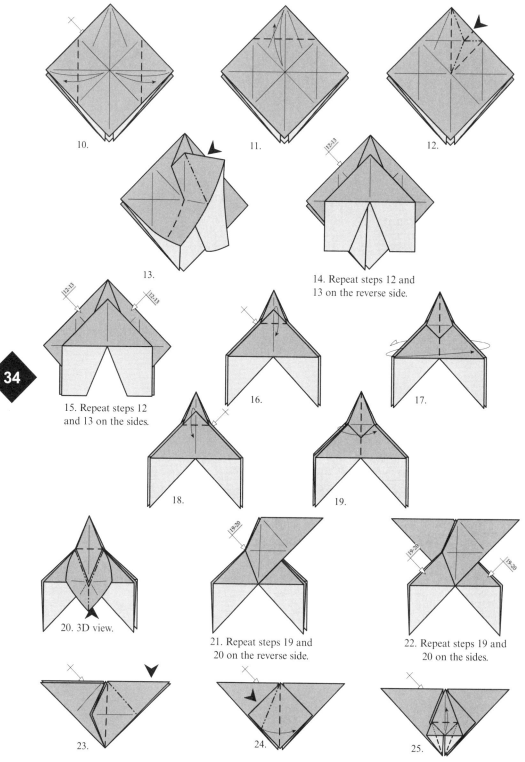

10.

11.

12.

13.

14. Repeat steps 12 and 13 on the reverse side.

34

15. Repeat steps 12 and 13 on the sides.

16.

17.

18.

19.

20. 3D view.

21. Repeat steps 19 and 20 on the reverse side.

22. Repeat steps 19 and 20 on the sides.

23.

24.

25.

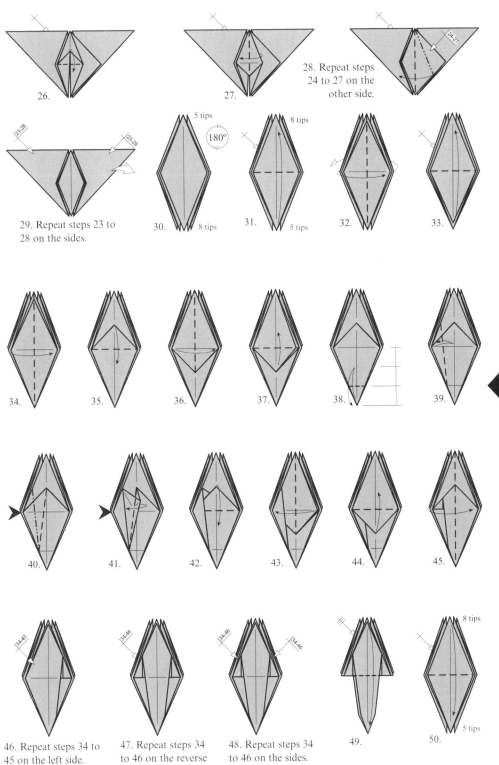

26.

27.

28. Repeat steps 24 to 27 on the other side.

29. Repeat steps 23 to 28 on the sides.

30.

5 tips

8 tips

180°

31.

8 tips

5 tips

32.

33.

34.

35.

36.

37.

38.

39.

35

40.

41.

42.

43.

44.

45.

46. Repeat steps 34 to 45 on the left side.

47. Repeat steps 34 to 46 on the reverse side.

48. Repeat steps 34 to 46 on the sides.

49.

50.

8 tips

5 tips

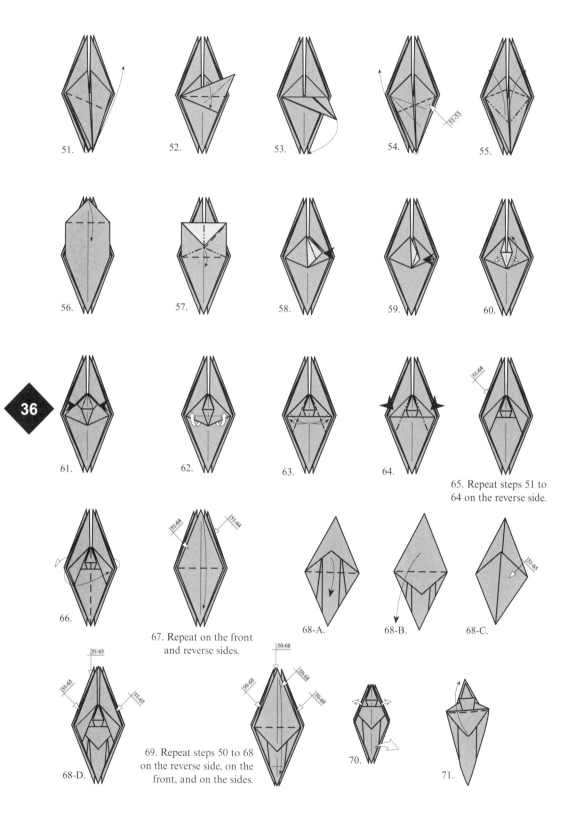

51.

52.

53.

54. 51-53

55.

56.

57.

58.

59.

60.

36

61.

62.

63.

64.

65. Repeat steps 51 to 64 on the reverse side.

66.

67. Repeat on the front and reverse sides.

68-A.

68-B.

68-C.

68-D.

69. Repeat steps 50 to 68 on the reverse side, on the front, and on the sides.

70.

71.

 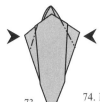 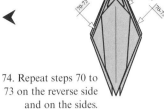

72.

73.

74. Repeat steps 70 to 73 on the reverse side and on the sides.

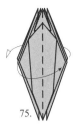

75.

   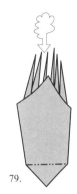

76.

77.

78. 3D view.

79.

HOW TO FOLD THE TENTACLES

Simple tentacles

Thick tentacles

Flat tentacles

80.

82. Double rabbit ear.

83. Double rabbit ear.

81.

Lobster

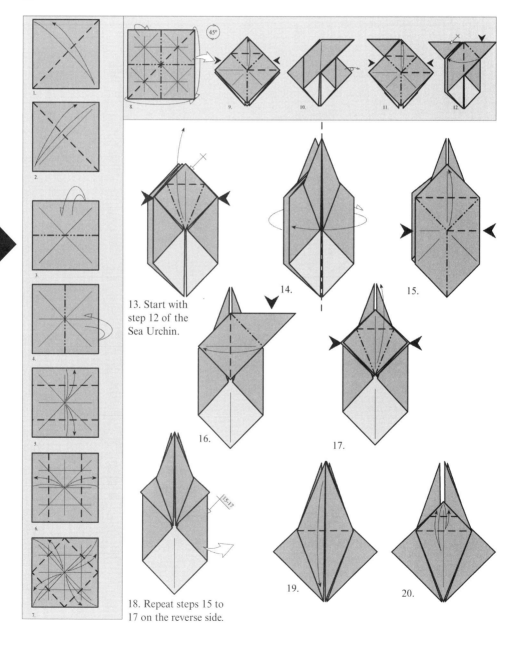

38

13. Start with step 12 of the Sea Urchin.

18. Repeat steps 15 to 17 on the reverse side.

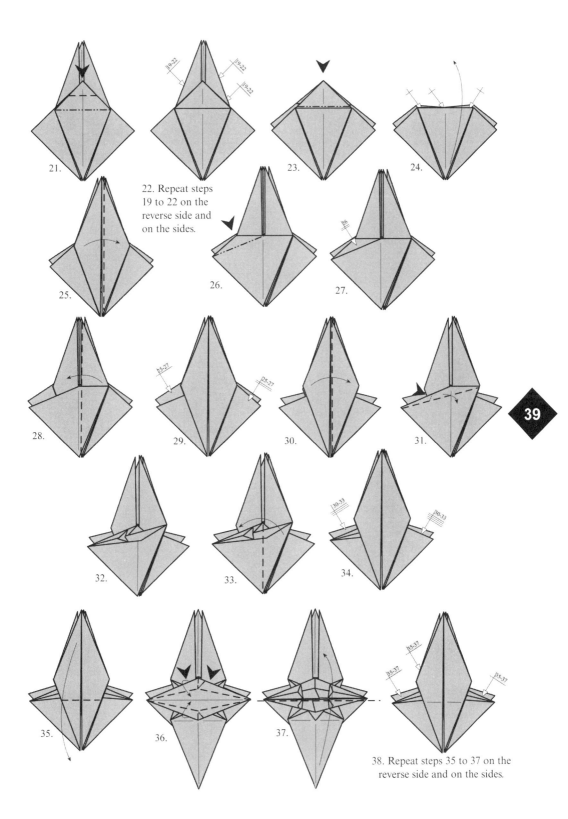

21.

22. Repeat steps 19 to 22 on the reverse side and on the sides.

23.

24.

25.

26.

27.

28.

29.

30.

31.

39

32.

33.

34.

35.

36.

37.

38. Repeat steps 35 to 37 on the reverse side and on the sides.

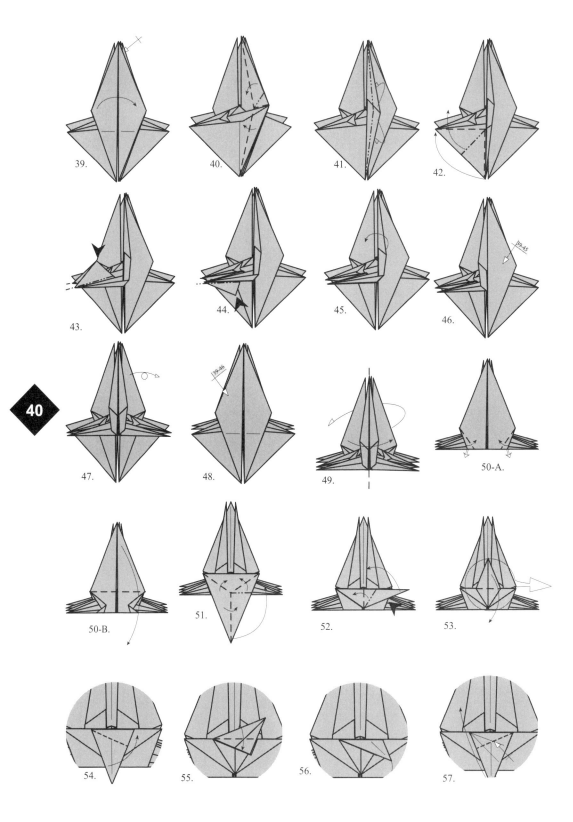

39.

40.

41.

42.

43.

44.

45.

46.

40

47.

48.

49.

50-A.

50-B.

51.

52.

53.

54.

55.

56.

57.

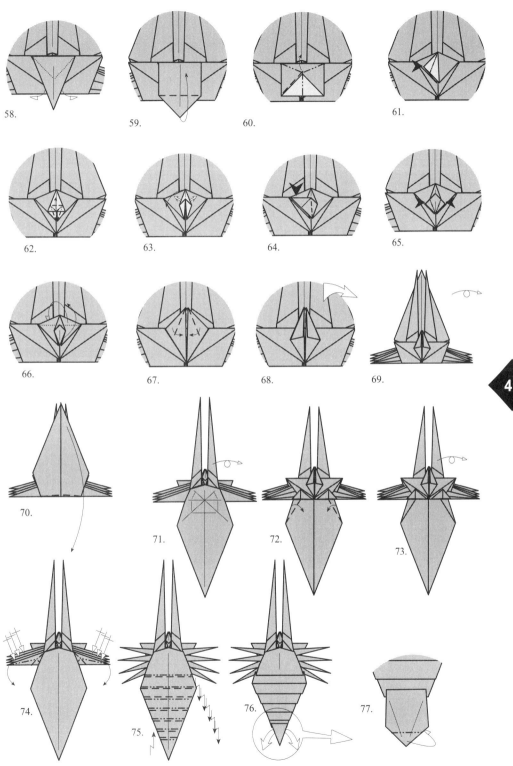

58.

59.

60.

61.

62.

63.

64.

65.

66.

67.

68.

69.

41

70.

71.

72.

73.

74.

75.

76.

77.

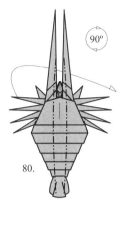

78.

79.

80.

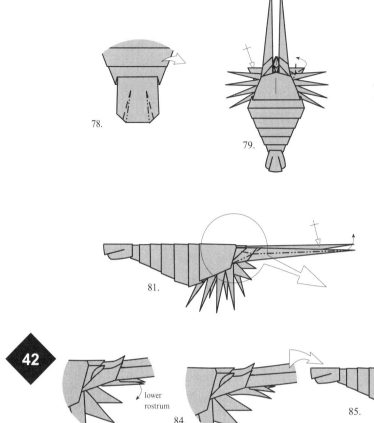

81.

82.

eyes   upper rostrum

83.

84.

85.

lower rostrum

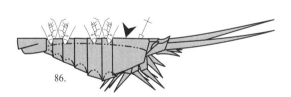

86.

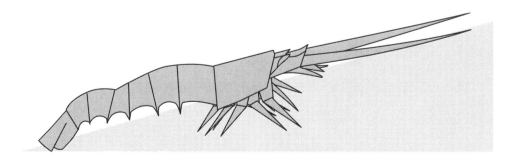

part

2

43

Sea Lion

1.

2.

3.

44

4.

5.

6.

7.

8.

9.

10.

11.

12.

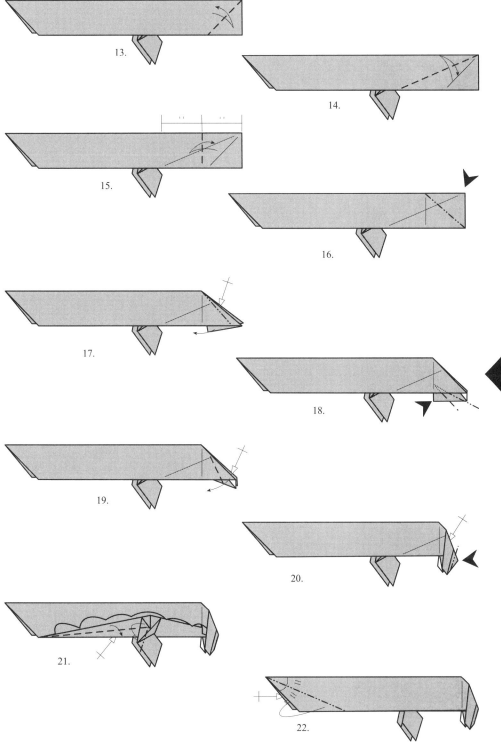

13.

14.

15.

16.

17.

18.

45

19.

20.

21.

22.

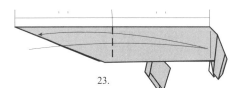

23.

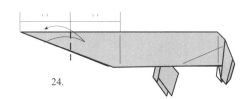

24.

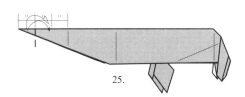

25.

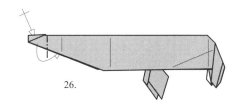

26.

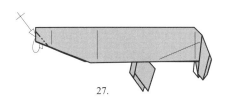

27.

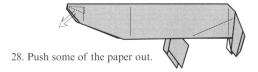

28. Push some of the paper out.

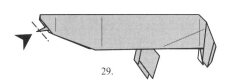

29.

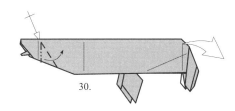

30.

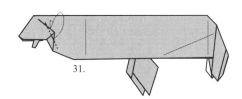

31.

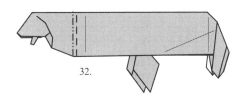

32.

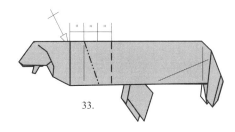

33.

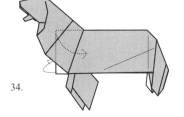

34.

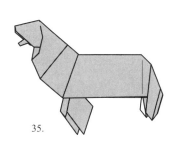

35.

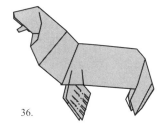

36.

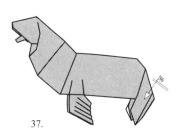

37.

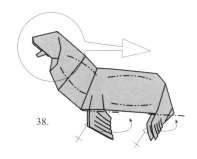

38.

39.

Walrus

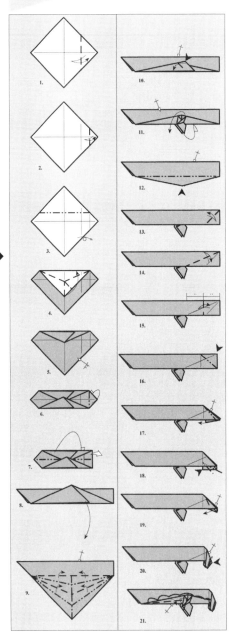

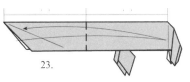

22. Start with step 21 of the Sea Lion.

23.

24.

25.

26.

27.

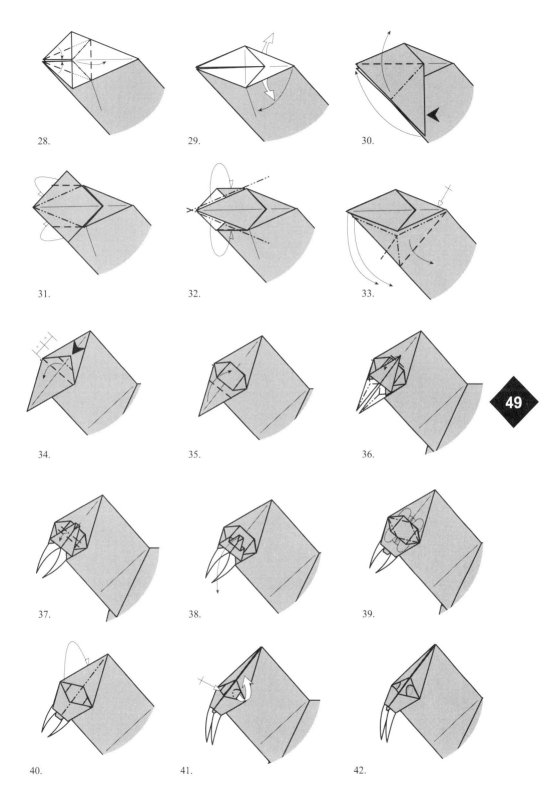

28.

29.

30.

31.

32.

33.

34.

35.

36.

49

37.

38.

39.

40.

41.

42.

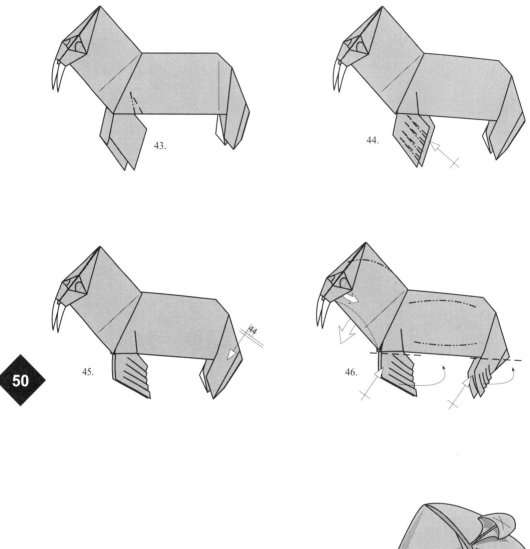

43.

44.

45.

46.

Manatee

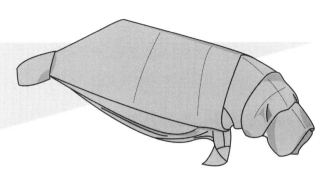

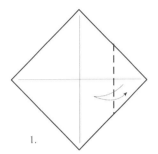

1.

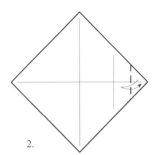

2.

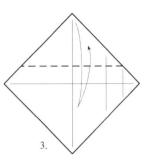

3.

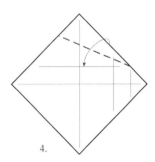

4.

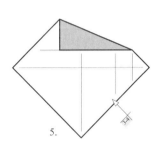

5.

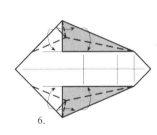

6.

51

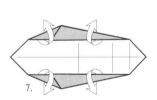

7.

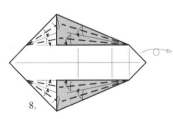

8.

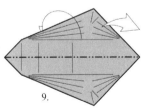

9.

10.

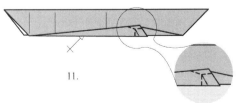

11.

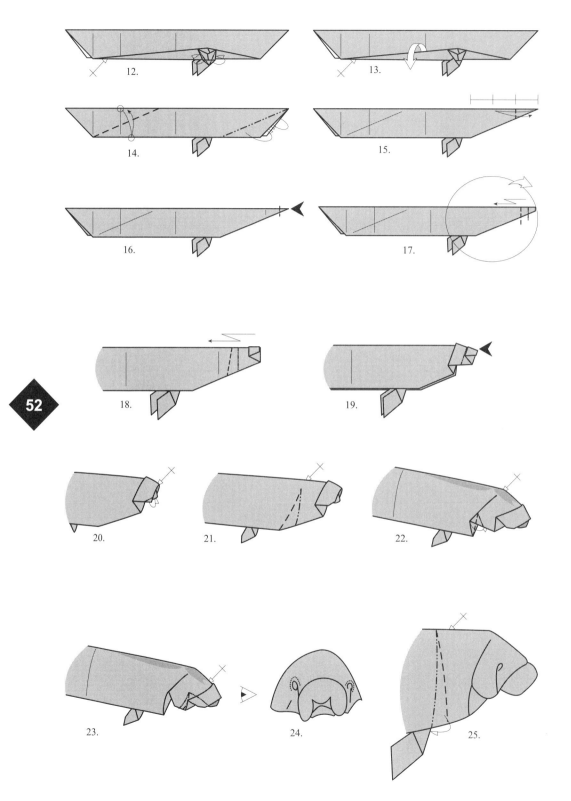

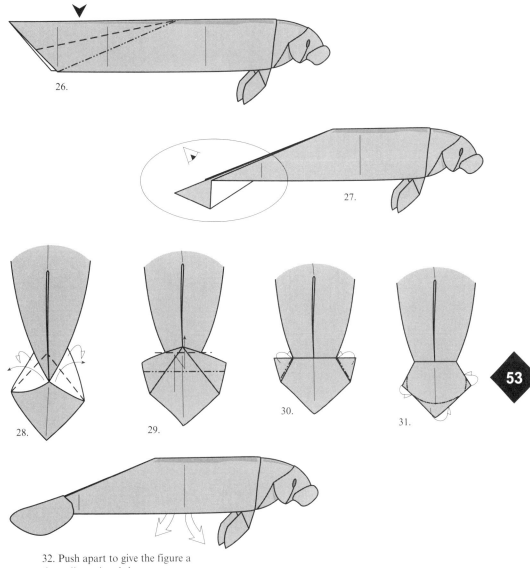

26.

27.

28.

29.

30.

31.

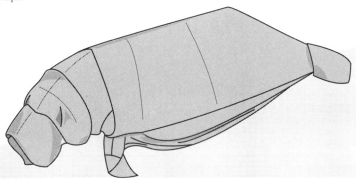

32. Push apart to give the figure a three-dimensional shape.

Polar Bear

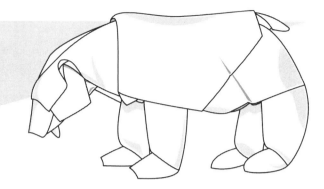

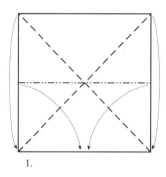

1.

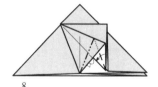

2.

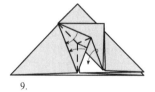

3.

54

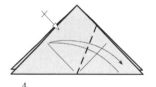

4.

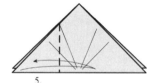

5.

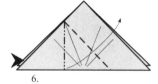

6.

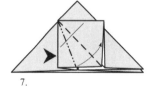

7.

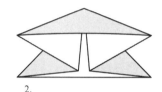

8.

9.

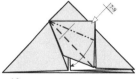

10.

11.

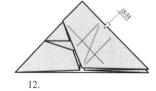

12.

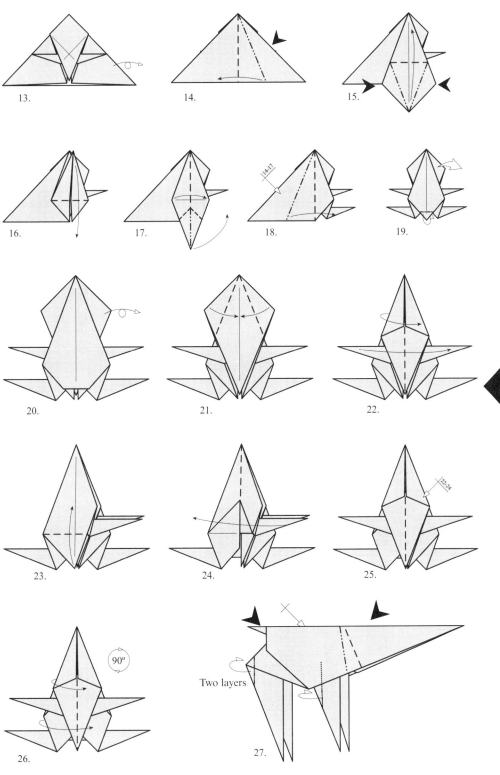

13.

14.

15.

16.

17.

18.

19.

20.

21.

22.

55

23.

24.

25.

26.

27.

90°

14-17

22-24

Two layers

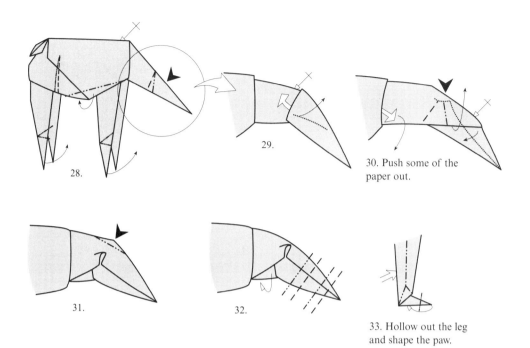

28.

29.

30. Push some of the paper out.

31.

32.

33. Hollow out the leg and shape the paw.

56

part 3

57

Centipede

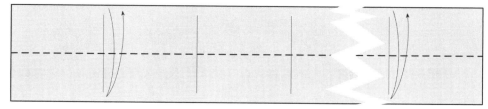

1. 1 x 21 rectangle.

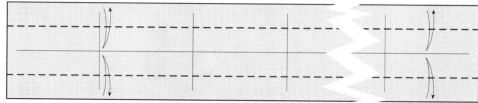

2.

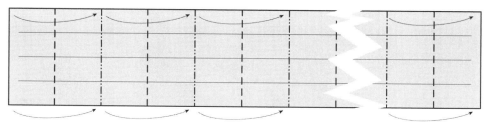

3. Fold to resemble the shape of an accordion.

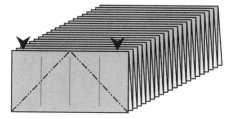

4. Repeat for all layers.

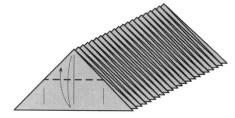

5. Repeat for all layers.

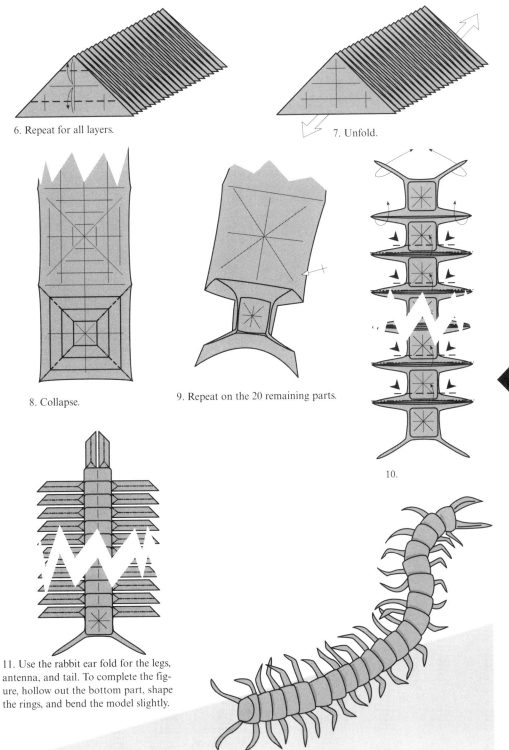

6. Repeat for all layers.

7. Unfold.

8. Collapse.

9. Repeat on the 20 remaining parts.

10.

59

11. Use the rabbit ear fold for the legs, antenna, and tail. To complete the figure, hollow out the bottom part, shape the rings, and bend the model slightly.

Timberman Beetle

1.

2.

3.

4.

5.

6.

7.

8.

9.

10.

11.

12.

13.

14.

15.

16.

17.

18. Start with step 18 of the Sea Urchin.

180°

19.

20.

21.

22.

23.

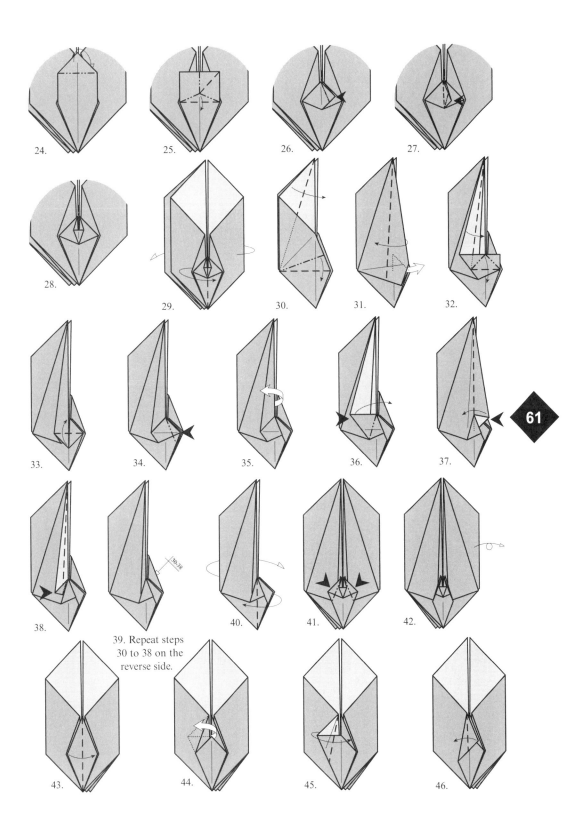

24.

25.

26.

27.

28.

29.

30.

31.

32.

33.

34.

35.

36.

37.

61

38.

39. Repeat steps 30 to 38 on the reverse side.

40.

41.

42.

30-38

43.

44.

45.

46.

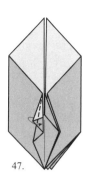

47.

48.

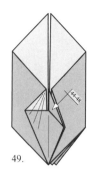

49.

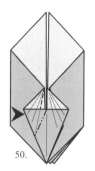

50.

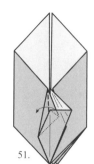

51.

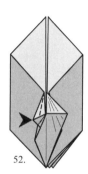

52.

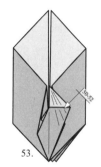

53.

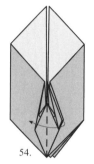

54.

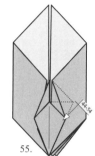

55.

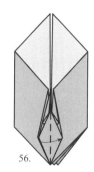

56.

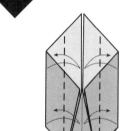

57.

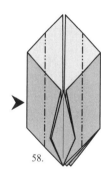

58.

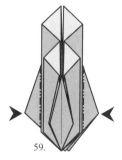

59.

60.

61.

62.

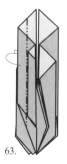

63.

64.

65.

62

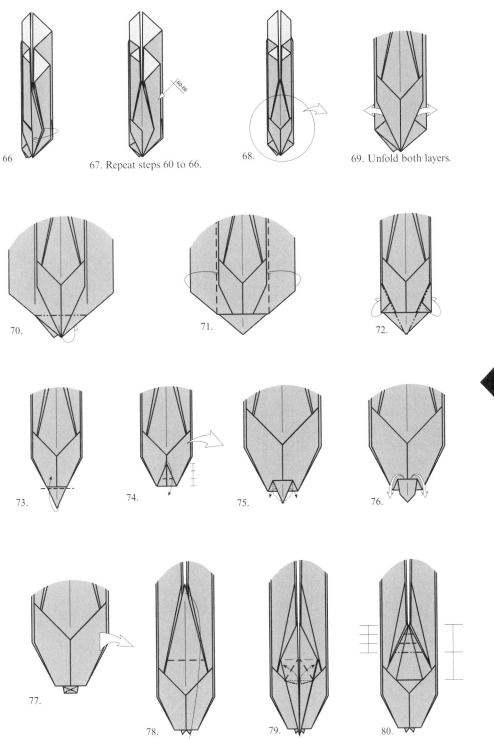

66

67. Repeat steps 60 to 66.

68.

69. Unfold both layers.

70.

71.

72.

73.

74.

75.

76.

77.

78.

79.

80.

63

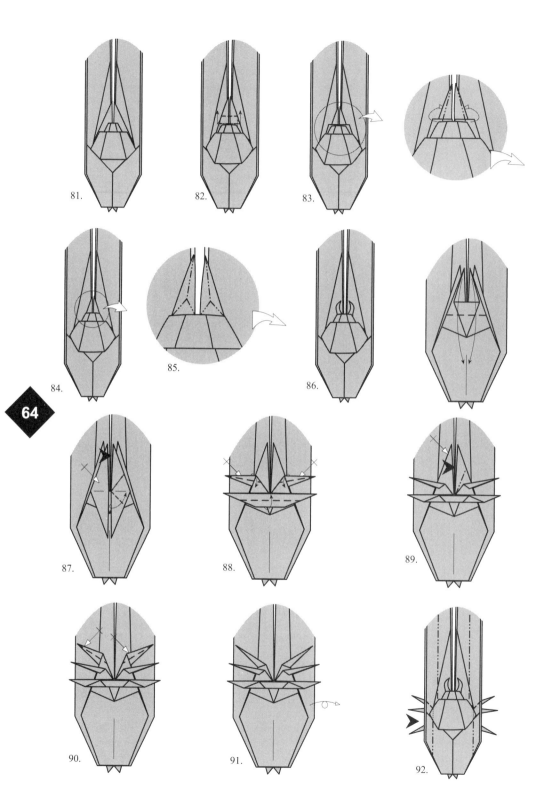

81.

82.

83.

84.

85.

86.

87.

88.

89.

90.

91.

92.

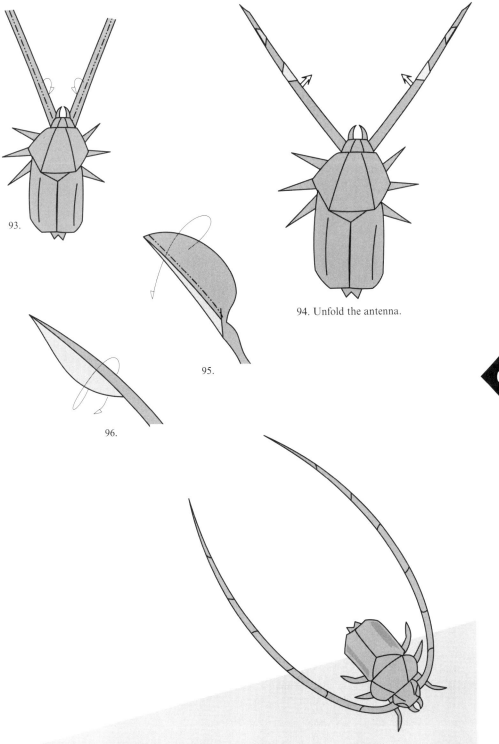

93.

94. Unfold the antenna.

95.

96.

Harlequin Beetle (Male)

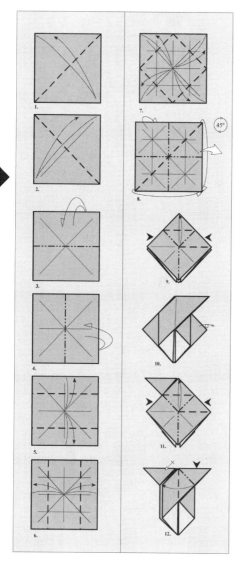

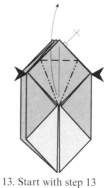

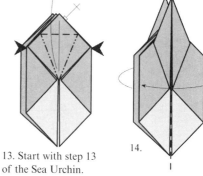

13. Start with step 13 of the Sea Urchin.

14.

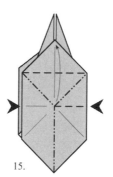

15.

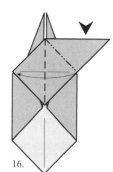

16.

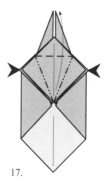

17.

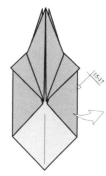

18. Repeat steps 15 to 17 on the reverse side.

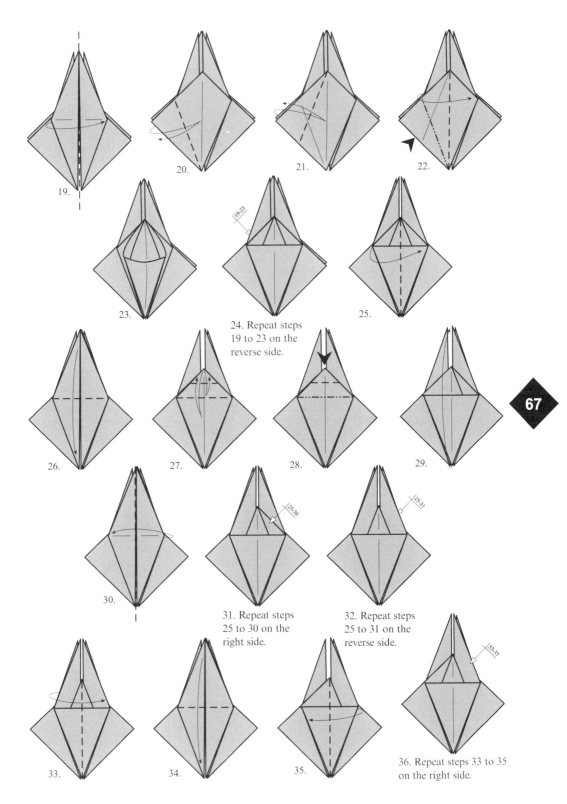

19.

20.

21.

22.

23.

24. Repeat steps
19 to 23 on the
reverse side.

25.

26.

27.

28.

29.

67

30.

31. Repeat steps
25 to 30 on the
right side.

32. Repeat steps
25 to 31 on the
reverse side.

33.

34.

35.

36. Repeat steps 33 to 35
on the right side.

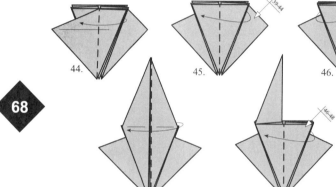

37. Repeat steps 33 to 36 on the reverse side.

38.

39.

40.

41. Sink fold.

42. Sink fold the second layer.

43. Sink fold the third layer.

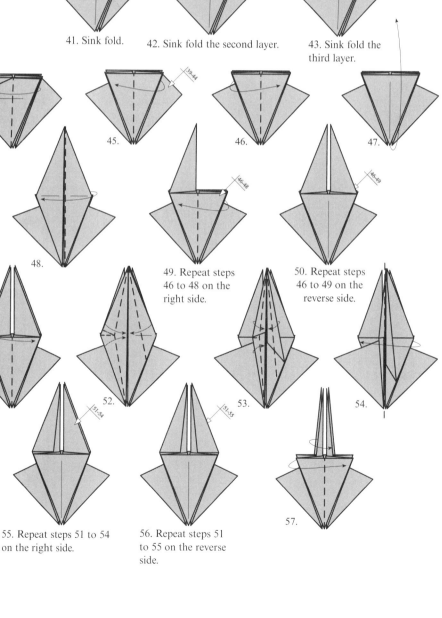

44.

45.

46.

47.

48.

49. Repeat steps 46 to 48 on the right side.

50. Repeat steps 46 to 49 on the reverse side.

51.

52.

53.

54.

55. Repeat steps 51 to 54 on the right side.

56. Repeat steps 51 to 55 on the reverse side.

57.

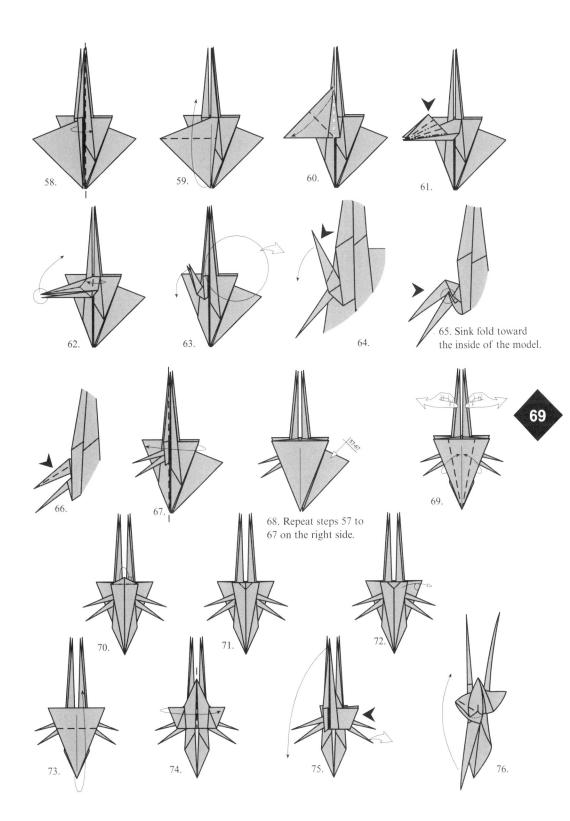

58.

59.

60.

61.

62.

63.

64.

65. Sink fold toward the inside of the model.

66.

67.

68. Repeat steps 57 to 67 on the right side.

69.

70.

71.

72.

73.

74.

75.

76.

69

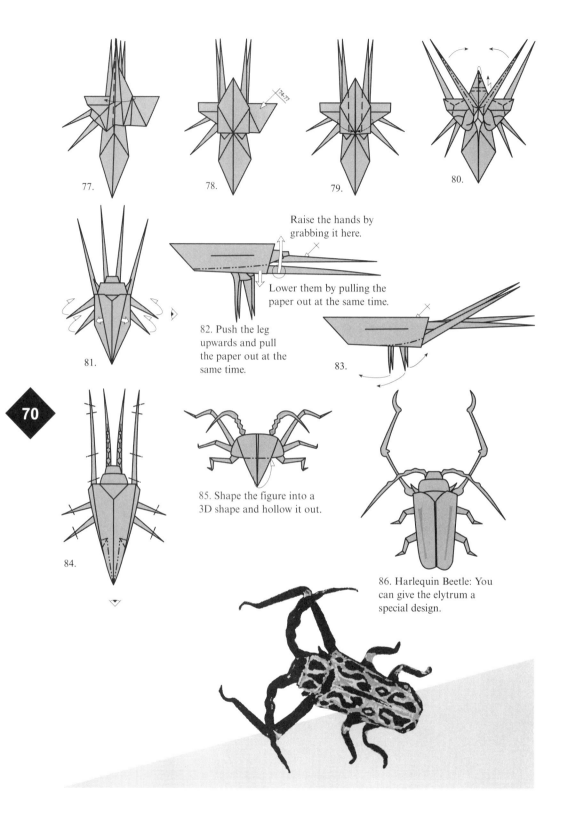

77.

78.

79.

80.

81.

Raise the hands by grabbing it here.

Lower them by pulling the paper out at the same time.

82. Push the leg upwards and pull the paper out at the same time.

83.

70

84.

85. Shape the figure into a 3D shape and hollow it out.

86. Harlequin Beetle: You can give the elytrum a special design.

Harlequin Beetle
(Female)

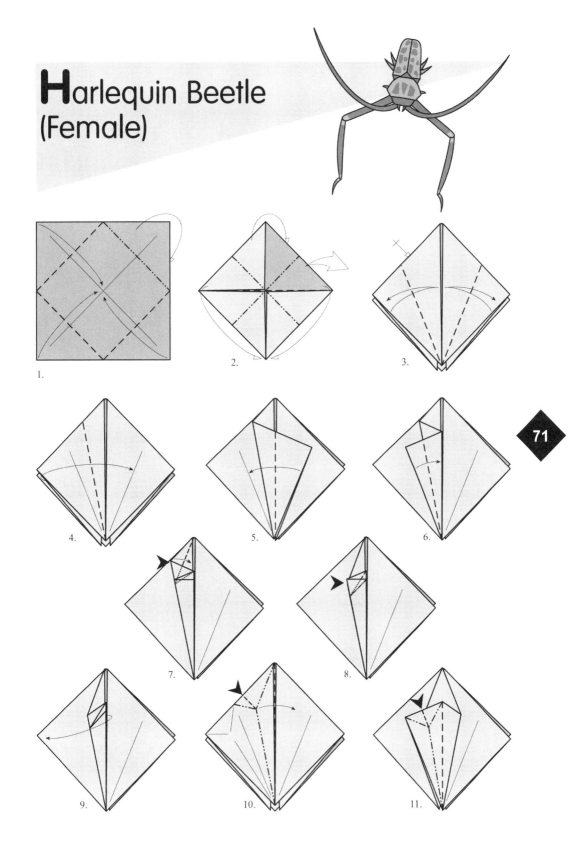

1.

2.

3.

4.

5.

6.

7.

8.

9.

10.

11.

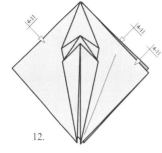

12.

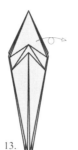

13.

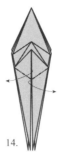

14.

15.

16.

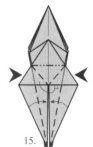

17.

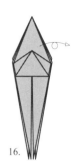

18.

19.

20.

21.

22.

23.

24.

25.

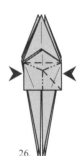

26.

27.

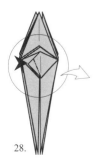

28.

29.

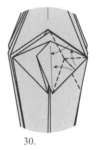

30.

31.

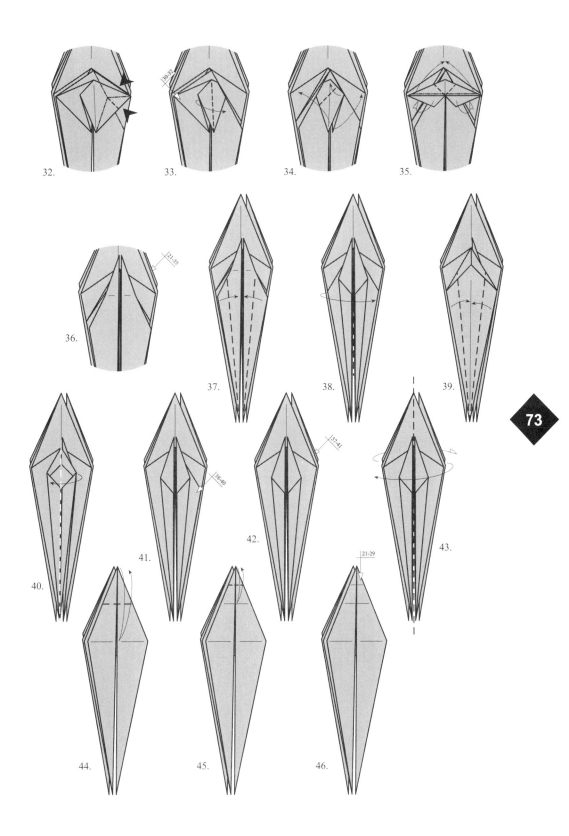

32.

33.

34.

35.

36.

37.

38.

39.

40.

41.

42.

43.

44.

45.

46.

73

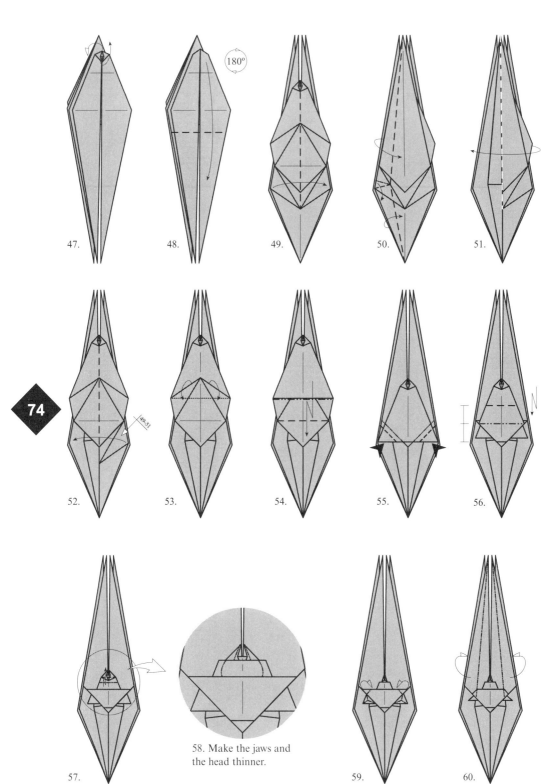

47.

48.

49.

50.

51.

74

52.

53.

54.

55.

56.

57.

58. Make the jaws and the head thinner.

59.

60.

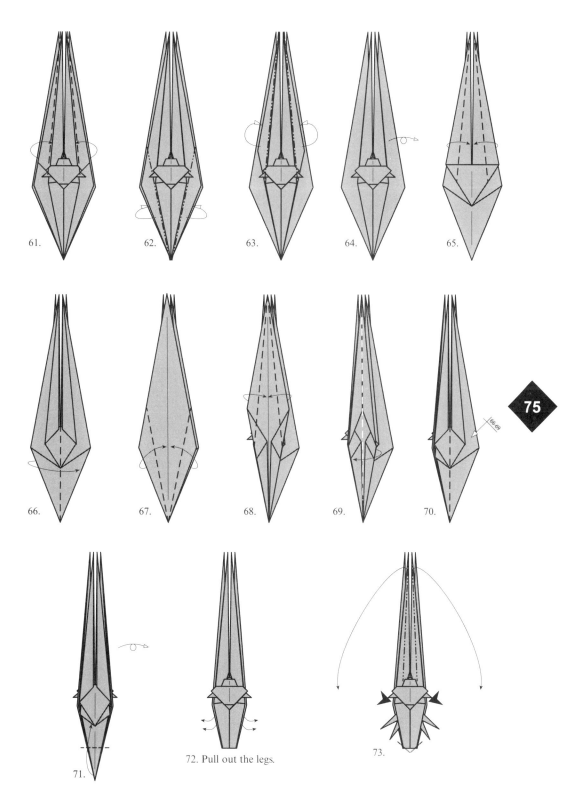

61.

62.

63.

64.

65.

66.

67.

68.

69.

70.

75

71.

72. Pull out the legs.

73.

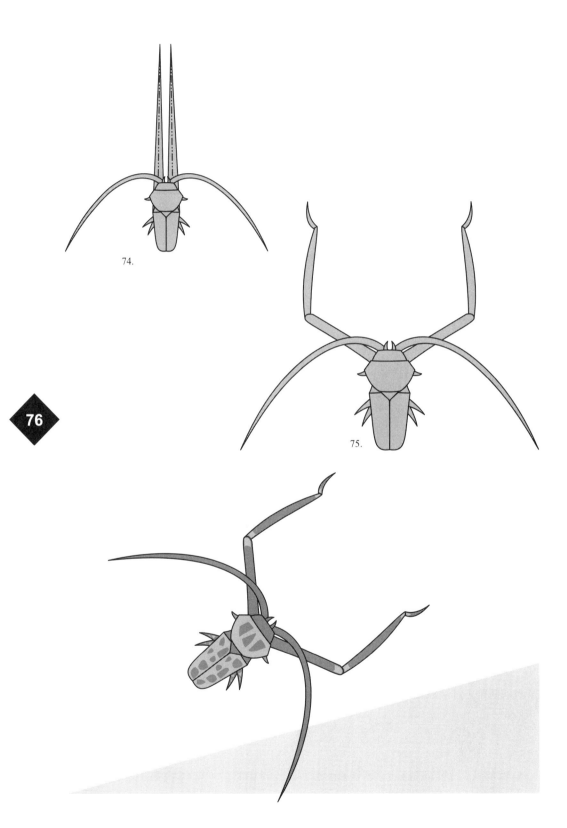

74.

75.

Stag Beetle

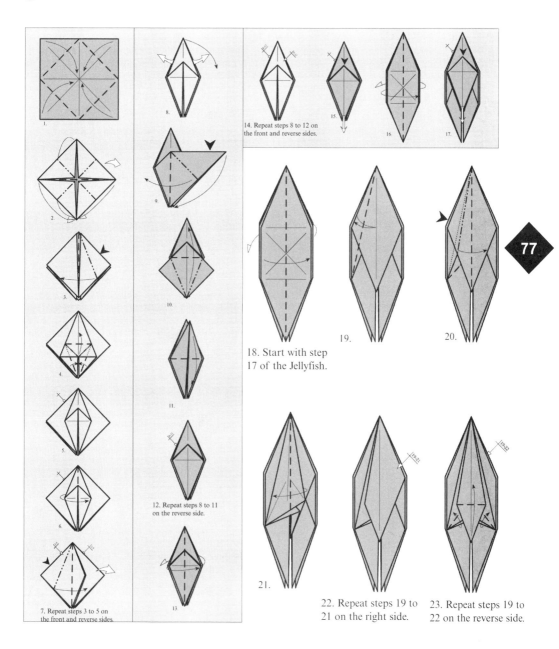

8.

9.

10.

11.

12. Repeat steps 8 to 11 on the reverse side.

13.

14. Repeat steps 8 to 12 on the front and reverse sides.

15.

16.

17.

18. Start with step 17 of the Jellyfish.

19.

20.

21.

22. Repeat steps 19 to 21 on the right side.

23. Repeat steps 19 to 22 on the reverse side.

1.

2.

3.

4.

5.

6.

7. Repeat steps 3 to 5 on the front and reverse sides.

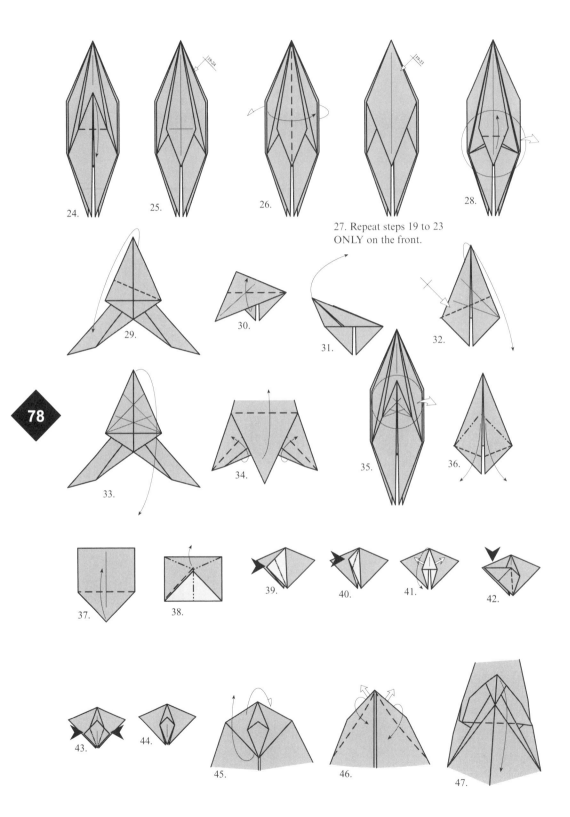

27. Repeat steps 19 to 23
ONLY on the front.

78

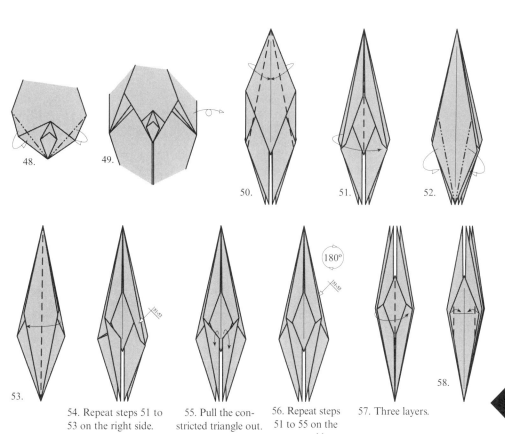

48.

49.

50.

51.

52.

53.

54. Repeat steps 51 to 53 on the right side.

55. Pull the constricted triangle out.

56. Repeat steps 51 to 55 on the reverse side. Rotate 180°.

57. Three layers.

58.

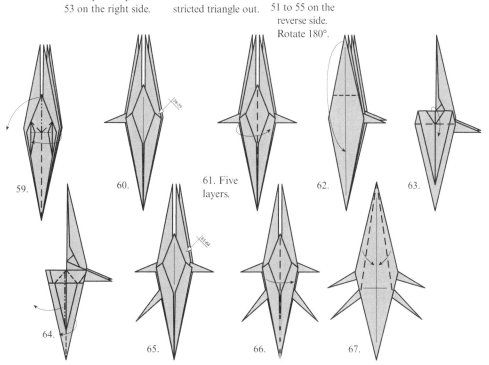

59.

60.

61. Five layers.

62.

63.

64.

65.

66.

67.

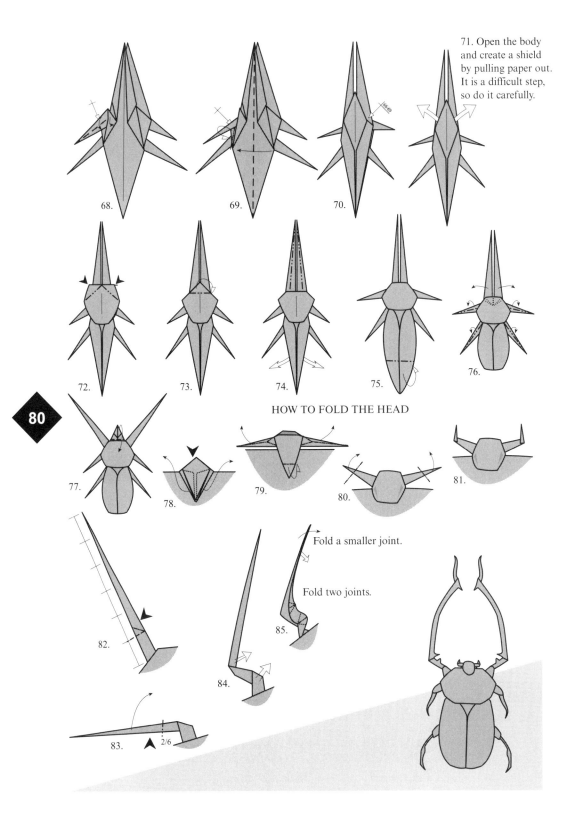

71. Open the body and create a shield by pulling paper out. It is a difficult step, so do it carefully.

68.

69.

70.

72.

73.

74.

75.

76.

80

77.

78.

79.

80.

81.

HOW TO FOLD THE HEAD

82.

83. 2/6

84.

85.

Fold a smaller joint.

Fold two joints.

Goliath Beetle

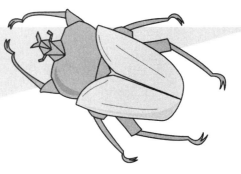

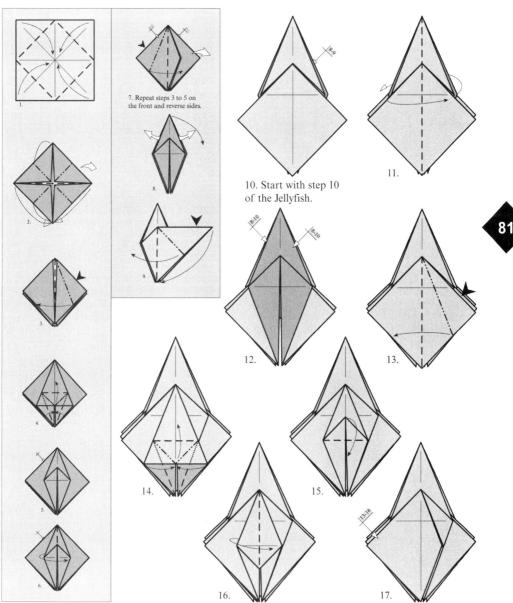

7. Repeat steps 3 to 5 on the front and reverse sides.

10. Start with step 10 of the Jellyfish.

1. 2. 3. 4. 5. 6. 8. 9. 11. 12. 13. 14. 15. 16. 17.

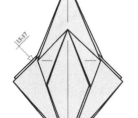

18.

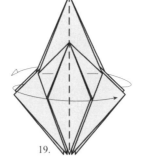

19.

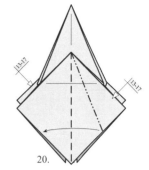

20.

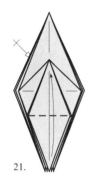

21.

22.

23.

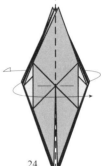

24.

25.

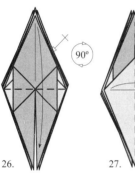

90°

26.

27.

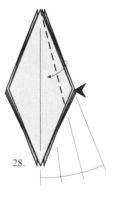

28.

29.

30.

31.

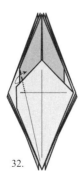

32.

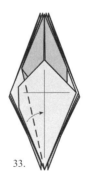

33.

34.

35.

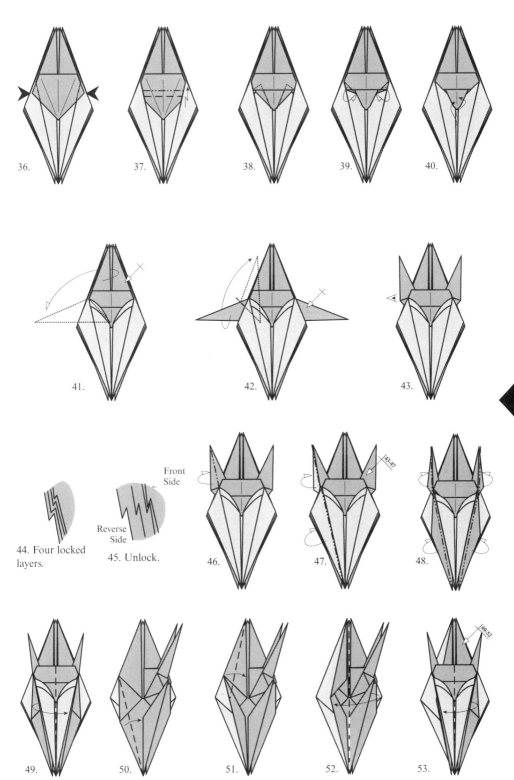

36.

37.

38.

39.

40.

41.

42.

43.

83

44. Four locked layers.

45. Unlock.

Front Side

Reverse Side

46.

47.

48.

49.

50.

51.

52.

53.

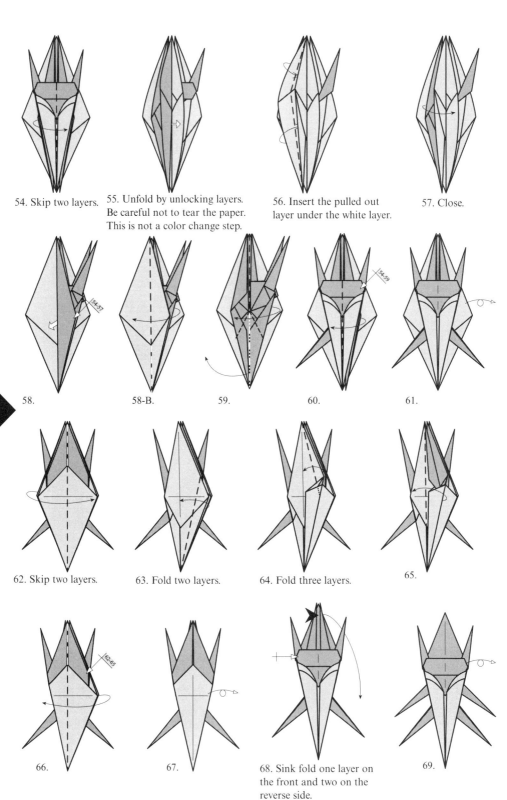

54. Skip two layers.

55. Unfold by unlocking layers. Be careful not to tear the paper. This is not a color change step.

56. Insert the pulled out layer under the white layer.

57. Close.

58.

58-B.

59.

60.

61.

62. Skip two layers.

63. Fold two layers.

64. Fold three layers.

65.

66.

67.

68. Sink fold one layer on the front and two on the reverse side.

69.

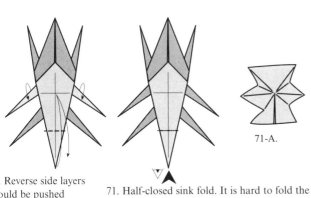

71-A.

(180°)

71-B. Pull out carefully. It is a hard but important step in order to hollow out the abdomen.

70. Reverse side layers should be pushed forward.

71. Half-closed sink fold. It is hard to fold the paper in this way. Do not open the model.

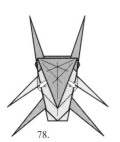

71-C.

71-D.

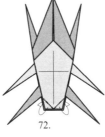

72.

73.

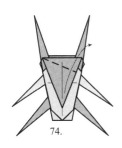

74.

75.

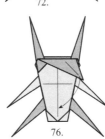

76.

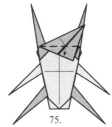

77.

85

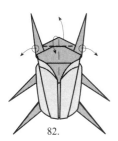

78.

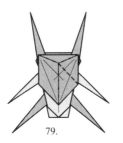

79.

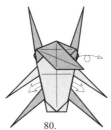

80.

81.

82.

83.

84.

85.

86.   87.   88.   89.

90.   91.   92.   93.

94.   95.   96.   97.

86

How to fold the legs

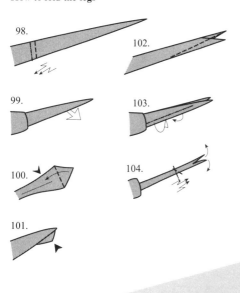

98.

99.

100.

101.

102.

103.

104.

Alpine Longhorn Beetle

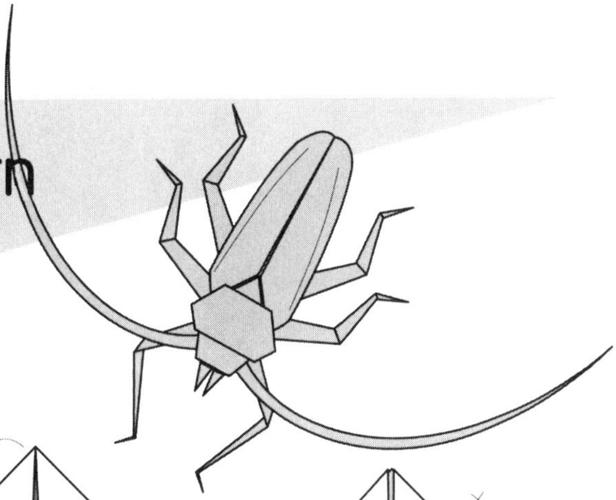

1.

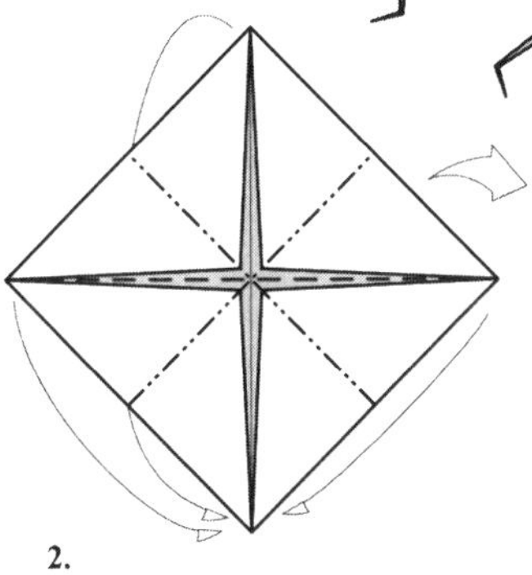

2.

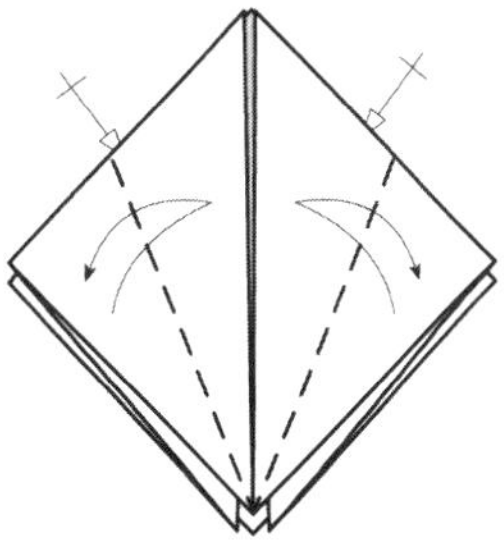

3.

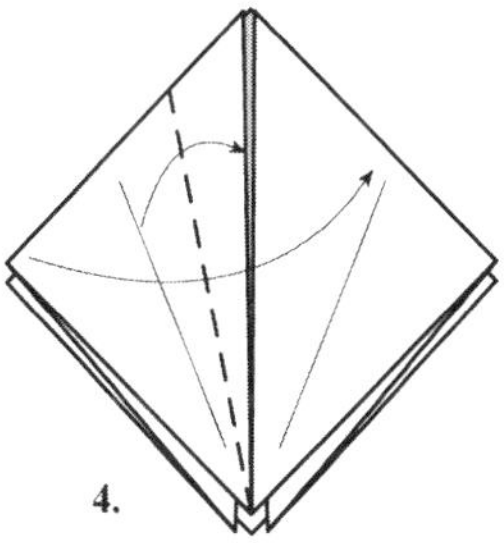

4.

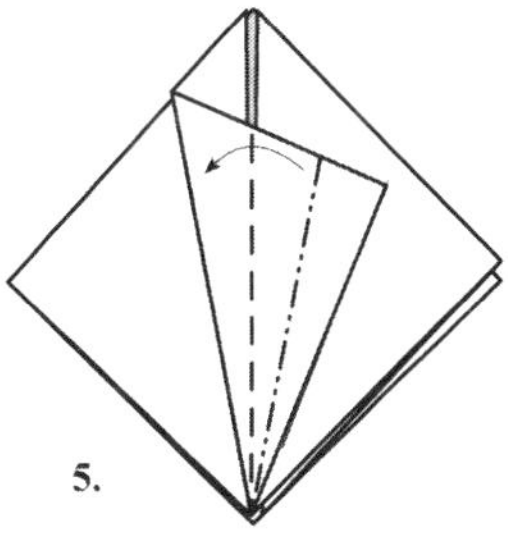

5.

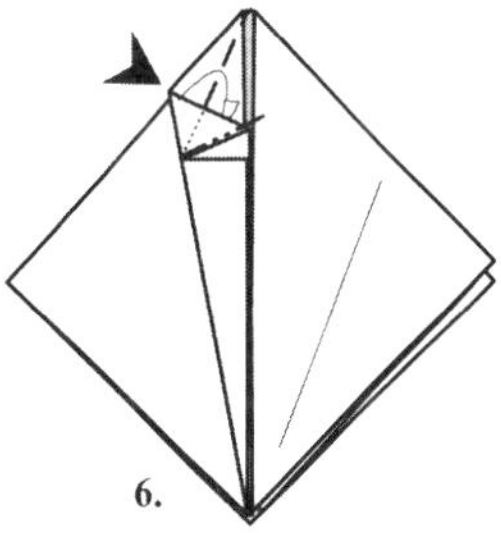

6.

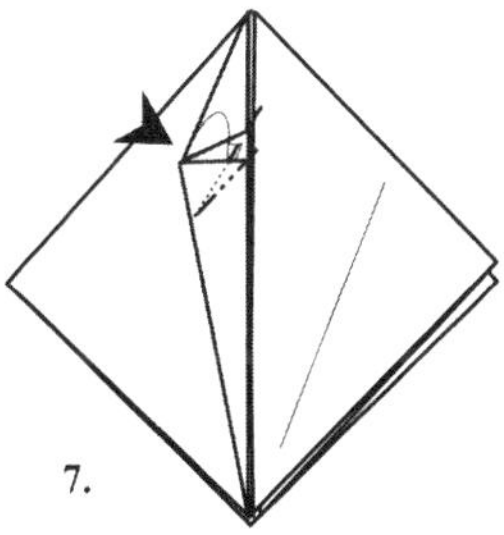

7.

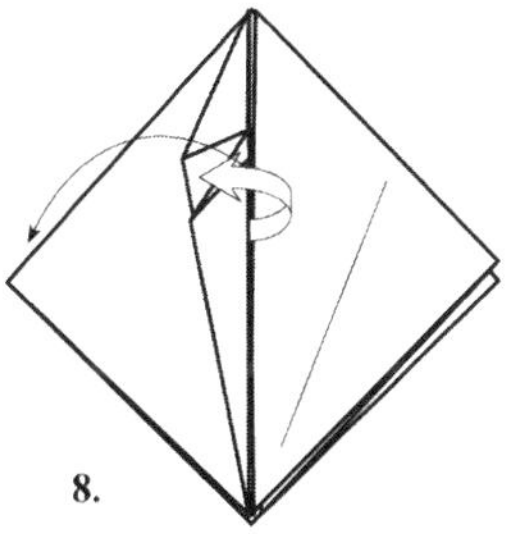

8.

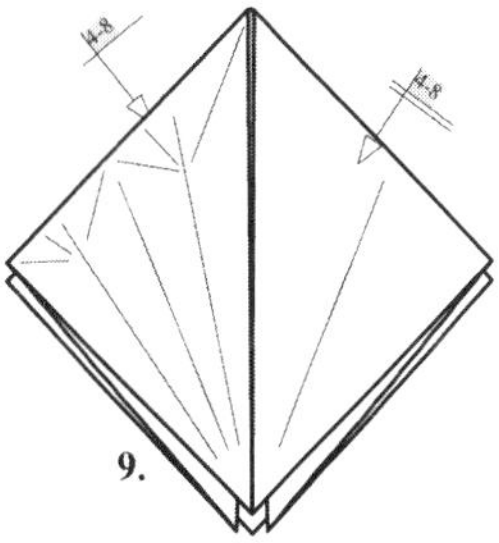

9. |4-8| |4-8|

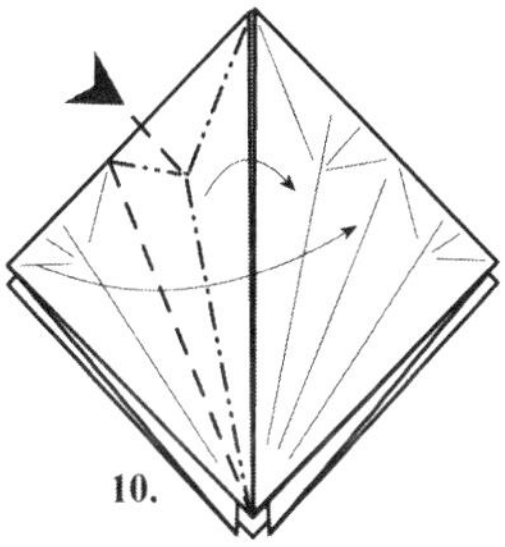

10.

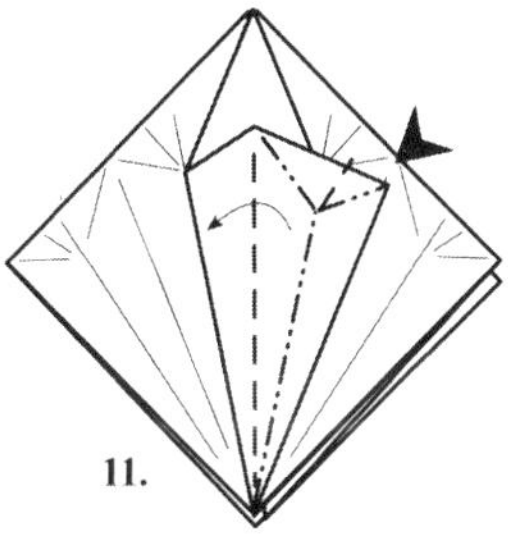

11.

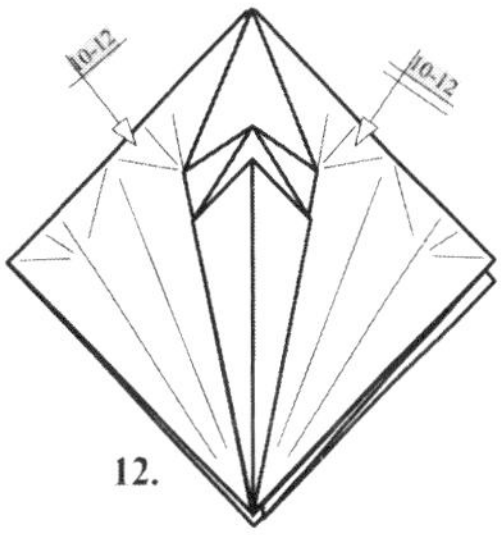

12. |0-12| |0-12|

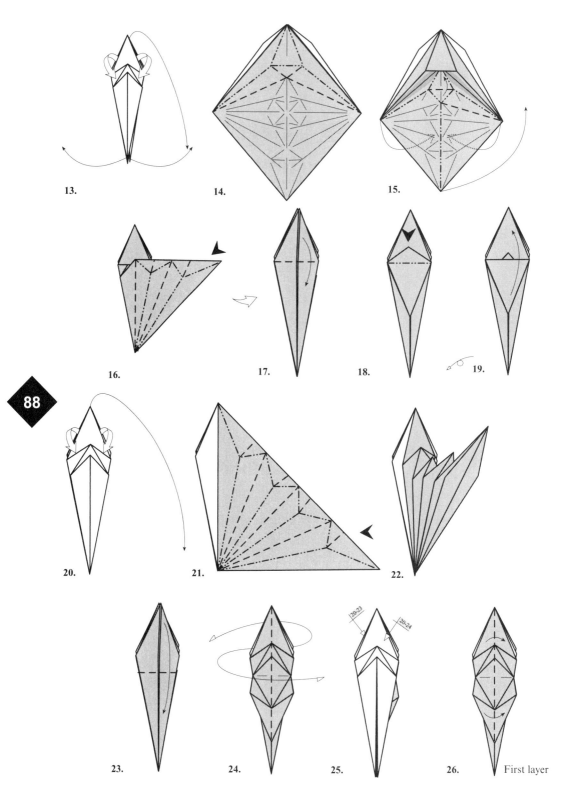

13.

14.

15.

16.

17.

18.

19.

88

20.

21.

22.

23.

24.

25.

26.   First layer

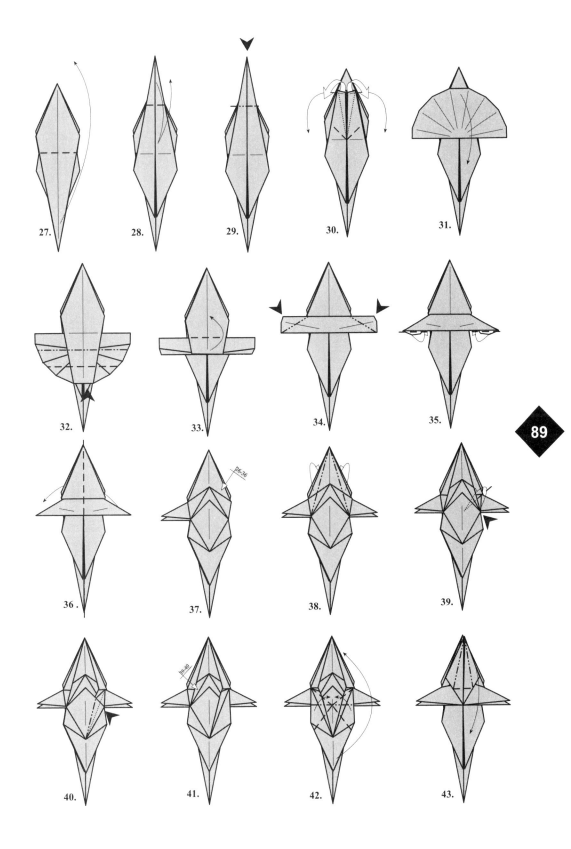

27.

28.

29.

30.

31.

32.

33.

34.

35.

89

36 .

37.

38.

39.

40.

41.

42.

43.

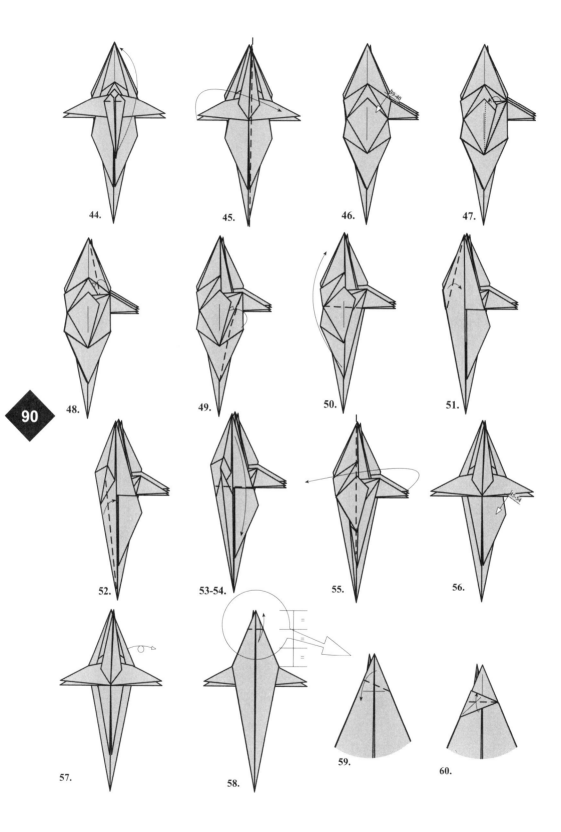

44.

45.

46.

47.

48.

49.

50.

51.

90

52.

53-54.

55.

56.

57.

58.

59.

60.

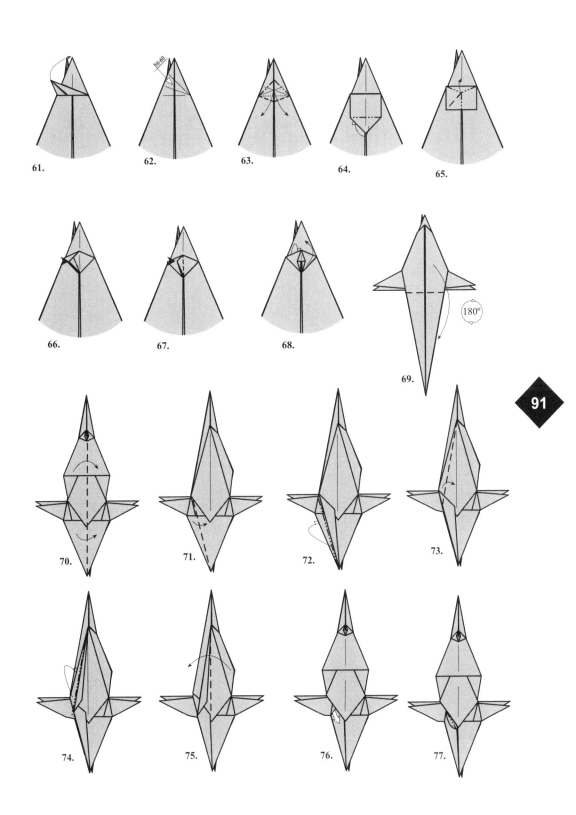

61.

62.

63.

64.

65.

66.

67.

68.

69.

180°

91

70.

71.

72.

73.

74.

75.

76.

77.

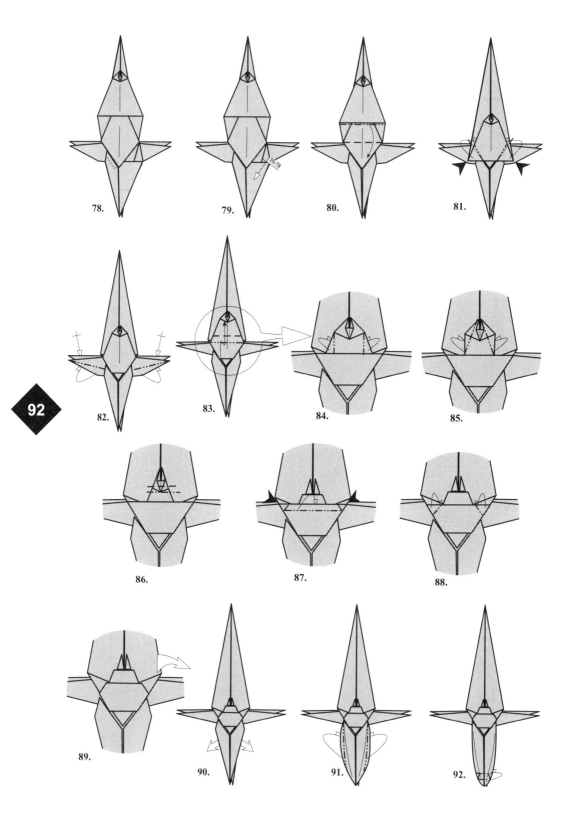

78.

79.

80.

81.

82.

83.

84.

85.

86.

87.

88.

89.

90.

91.

92.

92

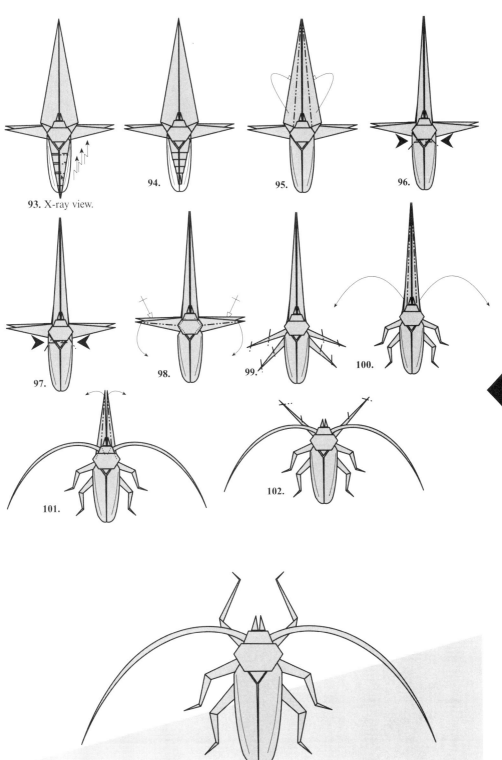

93. X-ray view.

94.

95.

96.

97.

98.

99.

100.

101.

102.

Migratory Locust

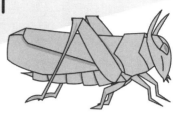

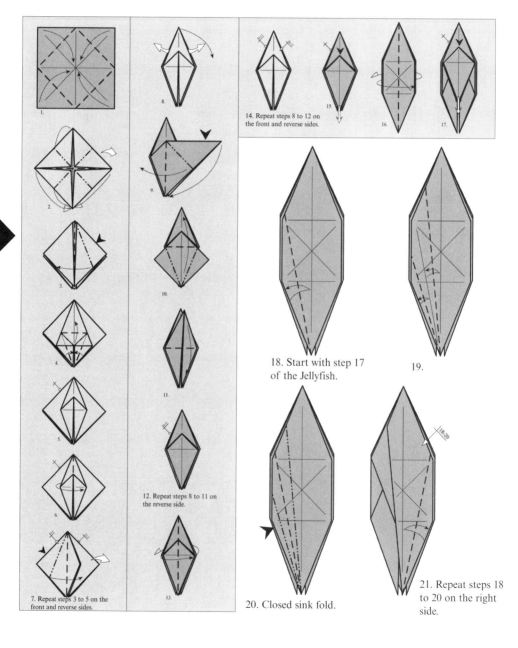

8.

9.

10.

11.

12. Repeat steps 8 to 11 on the reverse side.

13.

7. Repeat steps 3 to 5 on the front and reverse sides.

1.

2.

3.

4.

5.

6.

14. Repeat steps 8 to 12 on the front and reverse sides.

15.

16.

17.

18. Start with step 17 of the Jellyfish.

19.

20. Closed sink fold.

21. Repeat steps 18 to 20 on the right side.

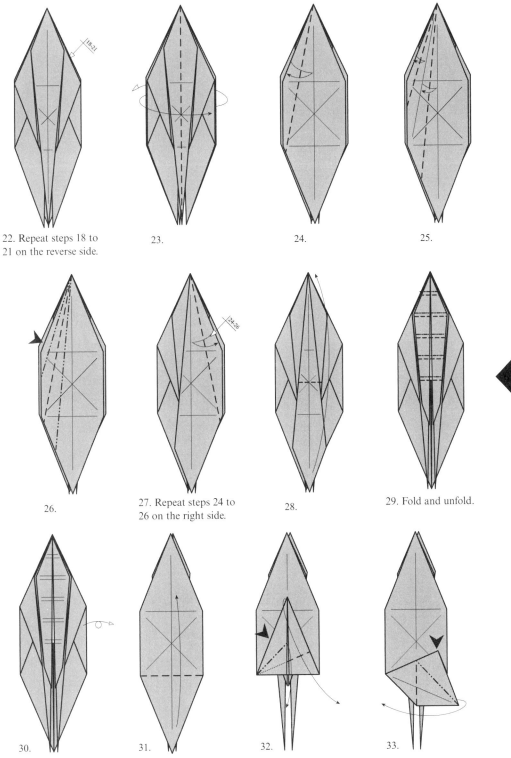

22. Repeat steps 18 to
21 on the reverse side.

23.

24.

25.

95

26.

27. Repeat steps 24 to
26 on the right side.

28.

29. Fold and unfold.

30.

31.

32.

33.

96

34.

35.

36.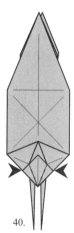

37.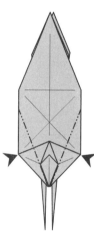

38.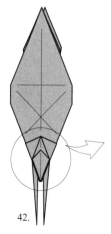

39.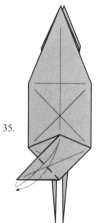

40.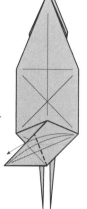

41. Closed sink fold.

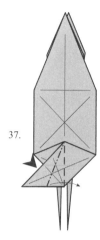

42.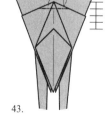

43.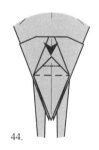

44.

45.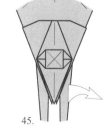

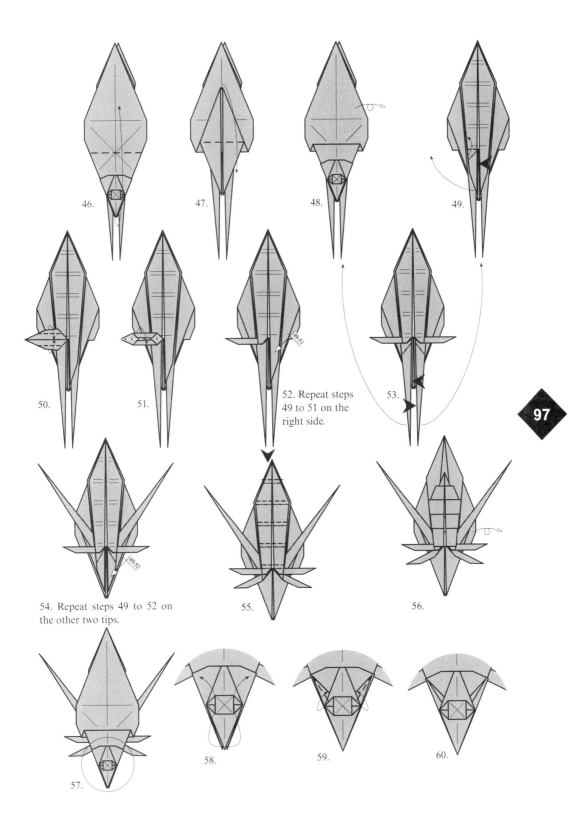

46.

47.

48.

49.

50.

51.

52. Repeat steps 49 to 51 on the right side.

53.

54. Repeat steps 49 to 52 on the other two tips.

55.

56.

57.

58.

59.

60.

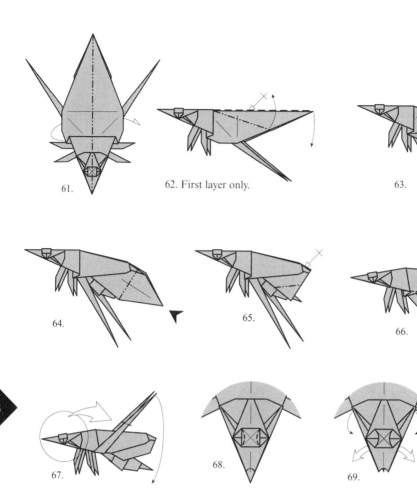

61.

62. First layer only.

63.

64.

65.

66.

67.

68.

69.

70.

Stick Grasshopper

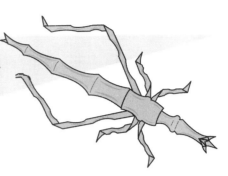

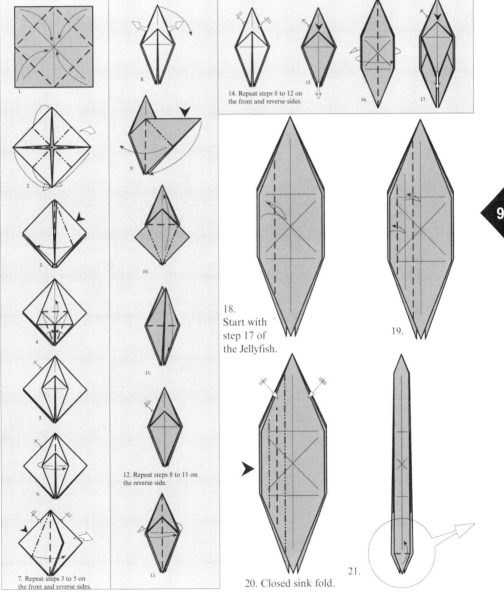

1.

2.

3.

4.

5.

6.

7. Repeat steps 3 to 5 on the front and reverse sides.

8.

9.

10.

11.

12. Repeat steps 8 to 11 on the reverse side.

13.

14. Repeat steps 8 to 12 on the front and reverse sides.

15.

16.

17.

18. Start with step 17 of the Jellyfish.

19.

20. Closed sink fold.

21.

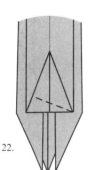

22.

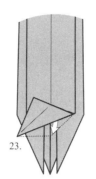

23.

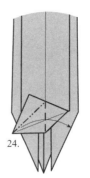

24.

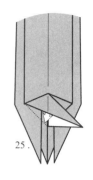

25.

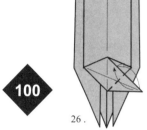

26.

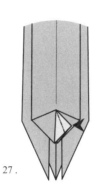

27.

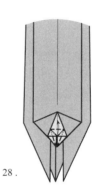

28.

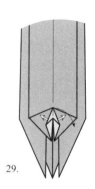

29.

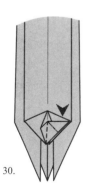

30.

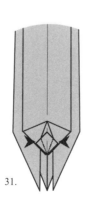

31.

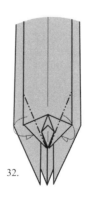

32.

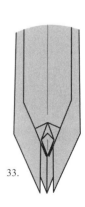

33.

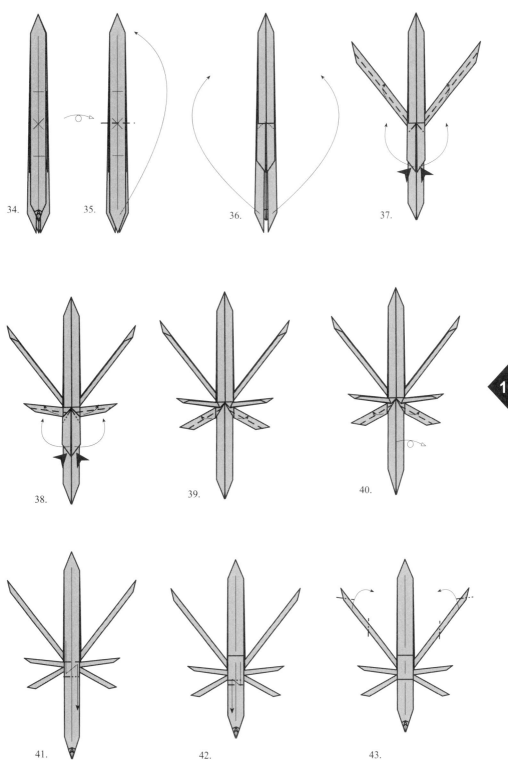

34.

35.

36.

37.

38.

39.

40.

101

41.

42.

43.

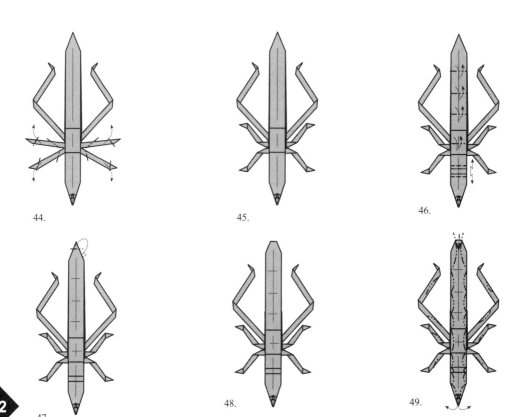

44.

45.

46.

47.

48.

49.

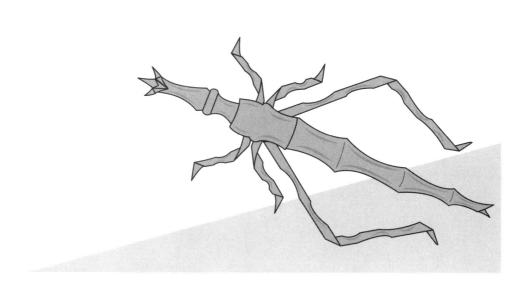

Giant Australian Earwig

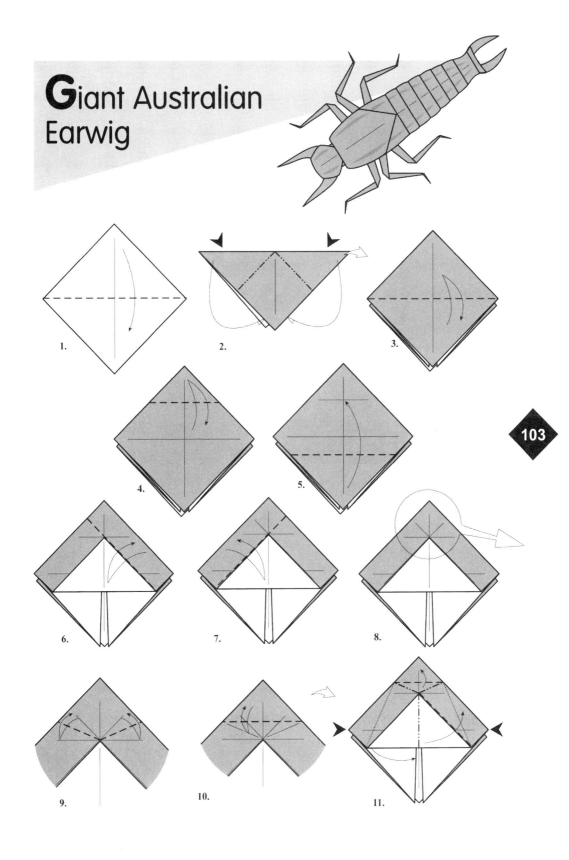

1.

2.

3.

4.

5.

6.

7.

8.

9.

10.

11.

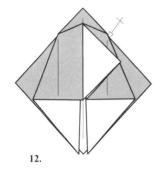

12.

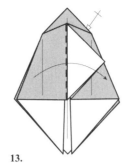

13.

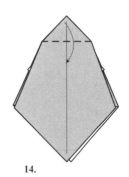

14.

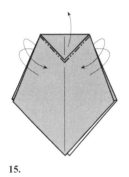

15.

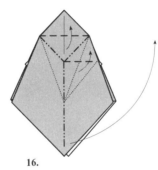

16.

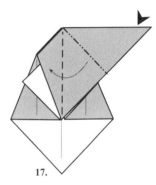

17.

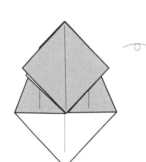

18.

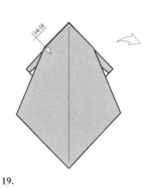

19.

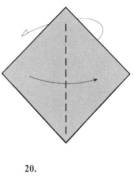

20.

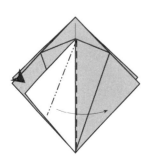

21.

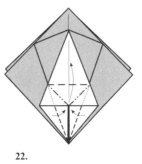

22.

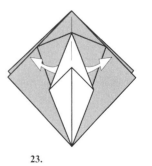

23.

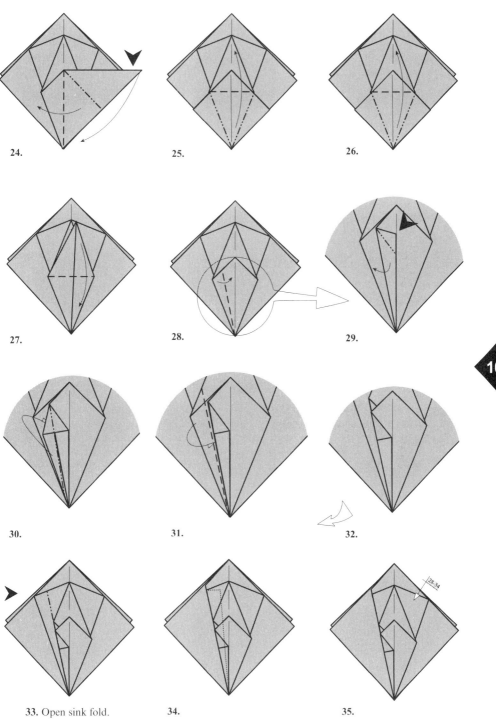

24.

25.

26.

27.

28.

29.

30.

31.

32.

33. Open sink fold.

34.

35.

105

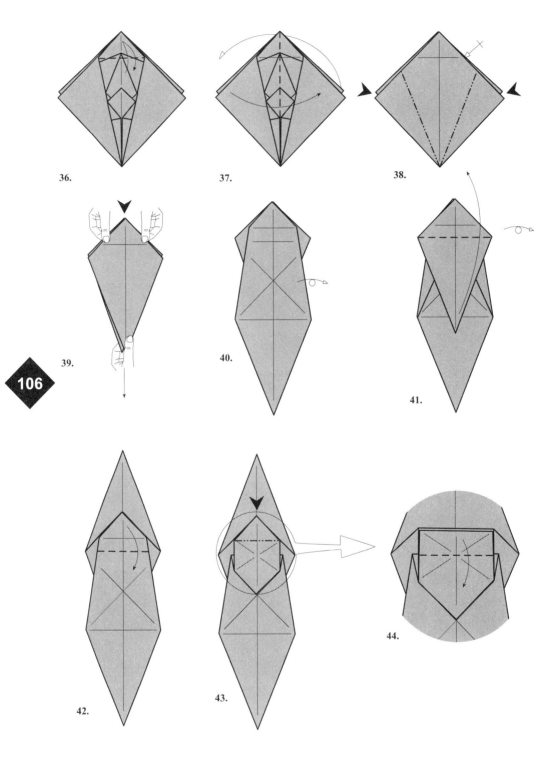

36.

37.

38.

39.

40.

41.

42.

43.

44.

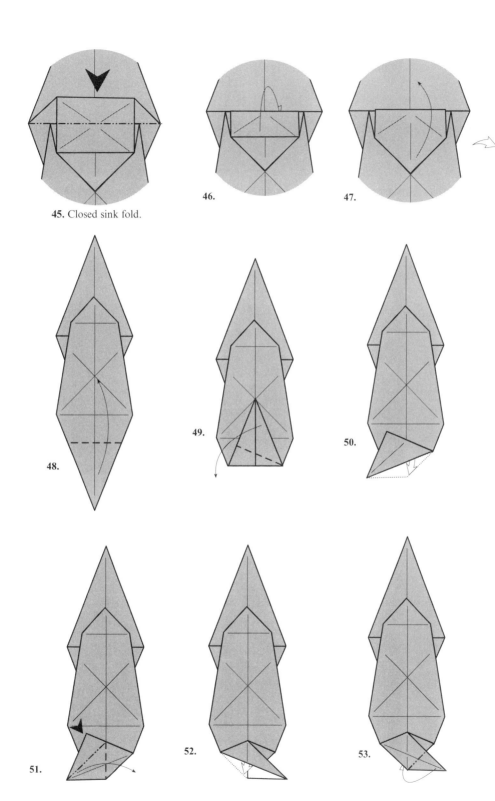

45. Closed sink fold.

46.

47.

48.

49.

50.

51.

52.

53.

107

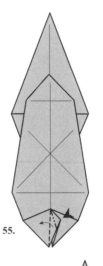

54.

55.

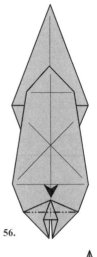

56.

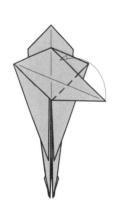

57.

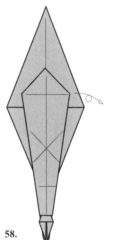

58.

49-53

59.

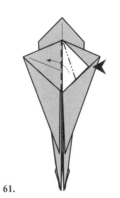

60.

61.

62.

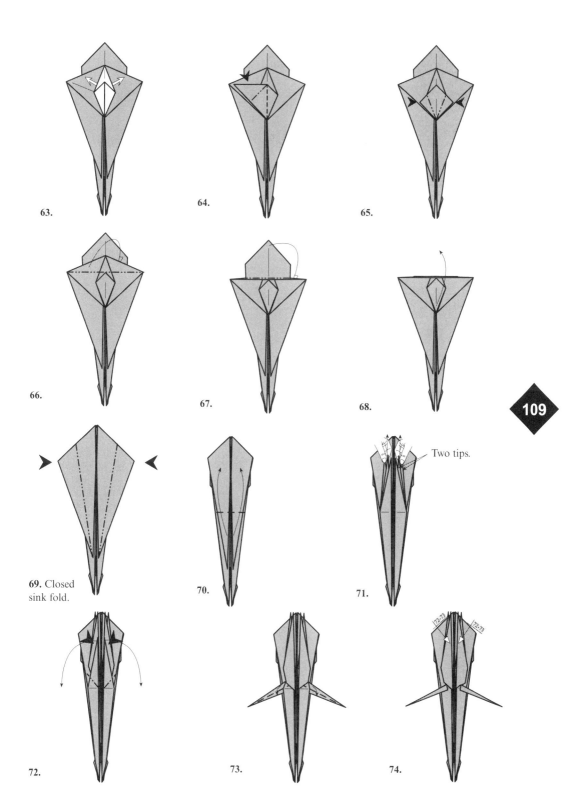

63.

64.

65.

66.

67.

68.

69. Closed sink fold.

70.

71. Two tips.

72.

73.

74.

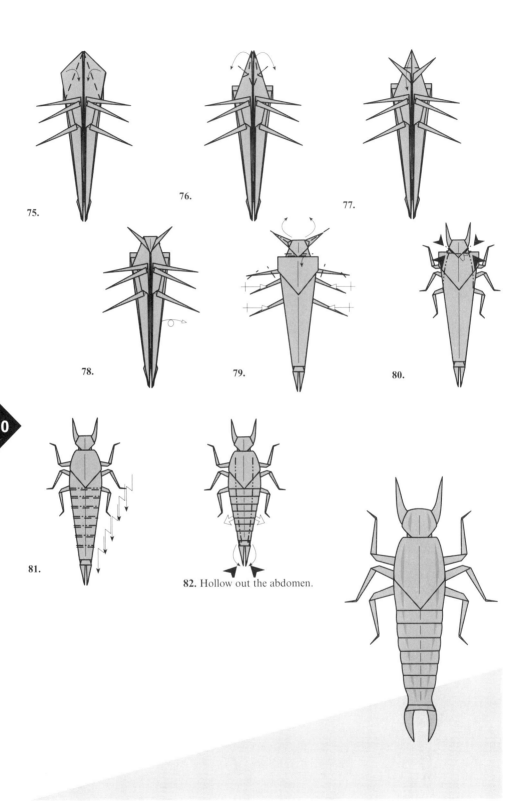

75.

76.

77.

78.

79.

80.

81.

82. Hollow out the abdomen.

Praying Mantis

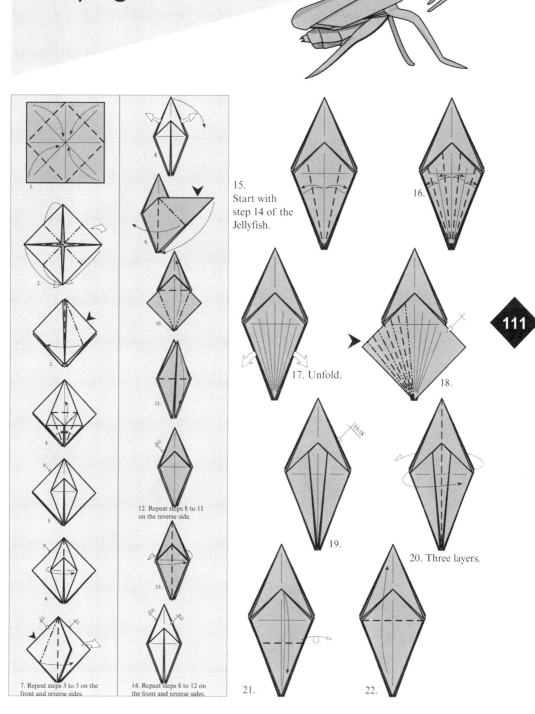

1.

2.

3.

4.

5.

6.

7. Repeat steps 3 to 5 on the front and reverse sides.

8.

9.

10.

11.

12. Repeat steps 8 to 11 on the reverse side.

13.

14. Repeat steps 8 to 12 on the front and reverse sides.

15. Start with step 14 of the Jellyfish.

16.

17. Unfold.

18.

19.

20. Three layers.

21.

22.

111

23.

24.

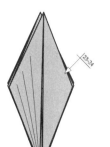

25.

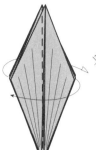

26. Two layers.

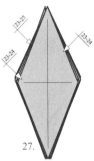

27.

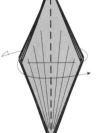

28. Four layers.

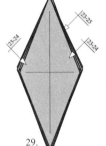

29.

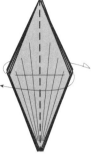

30. Two layers.

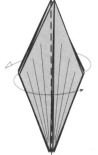

31. Three layers.

32.

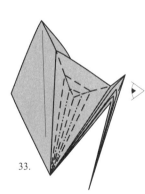

33.

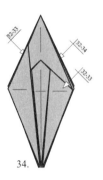

34.

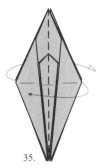

35.

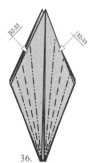

36.

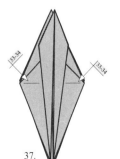

37.

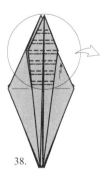

38.

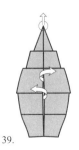

39.

40.

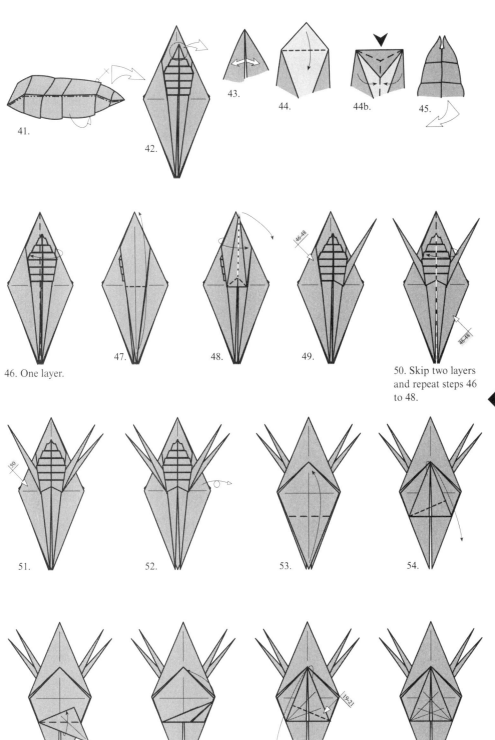

41.

42.

43.

44.

44b.

45.

46. One layer.

47.

48.

49.

50. Skip two layers and repeat steps 46 to 48.

113

51.

52.

53.

54.

55.

56.

57.

58.

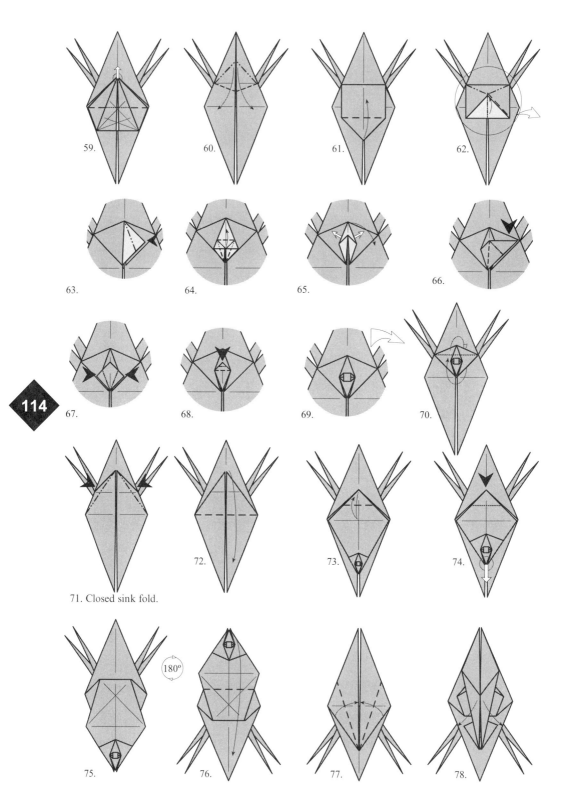

59.

60.

61.

62.

63.

64.

65.

66.

67.

68.

69.

70.

71. Closed sink fold.

72.

73.

74.

75.

76.

77.

78.

180°

114

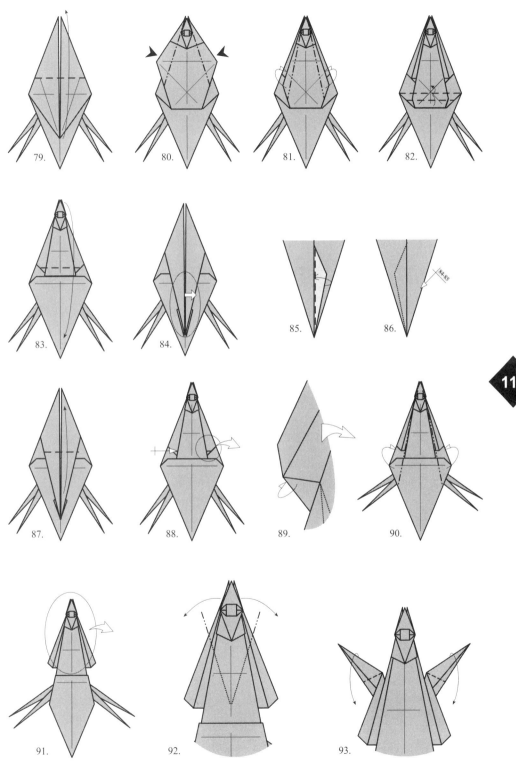

79.

80.

81.

82.

83.

84.

85.

86. 84-85

87.

88.

89.

90.

91.

92.

93.

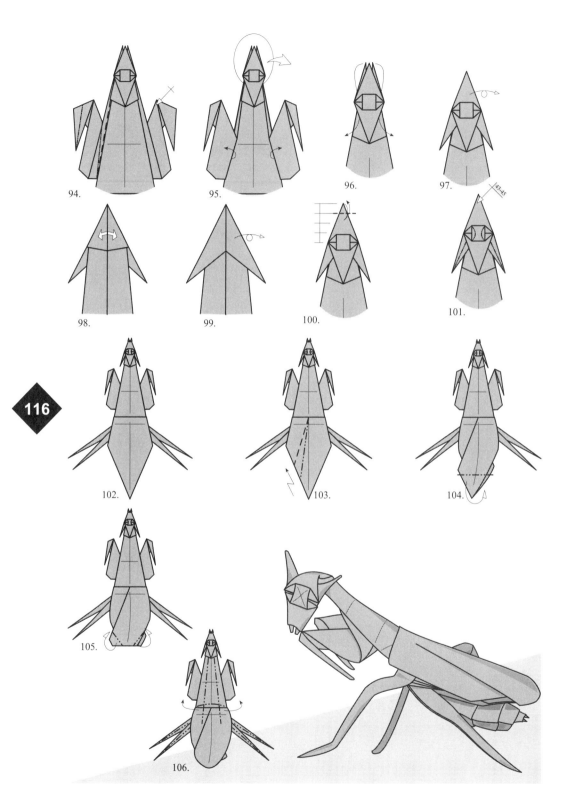

94.

95.

96.

97.

98.

99.

100.

101.

102.

103.

104.

105.

106.

"Little Devil" Mantid

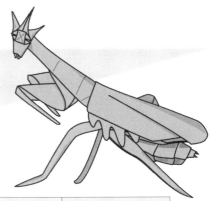

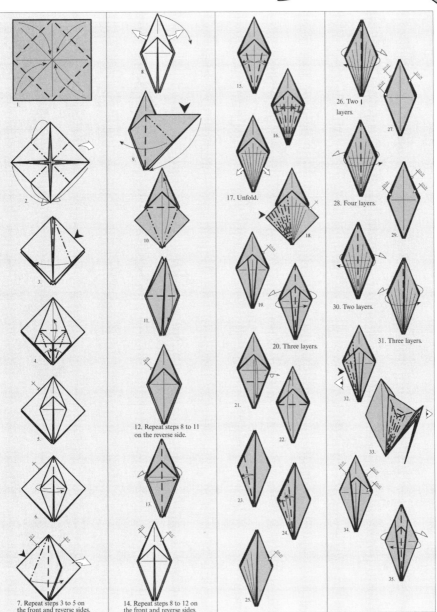

1.

2.

3.

4.

5.

6.

7. Repeat steps 3 to 5 on the front and reverse sides.

8.

9.

10.

11.

12. Repeat steps 8 to 11 on the reverse side.

13.

14. Repeat steps 8 to 12 on the front and reverse sides.

15.

16.

17. Unfold.

18.

19.

20. Three layers.

21.

22.

23.

24.

25.

26. Two layers.

27.

28. Four layers.

29.

30. Two layers.

31. Three layers.

32.

33.

34.

35.

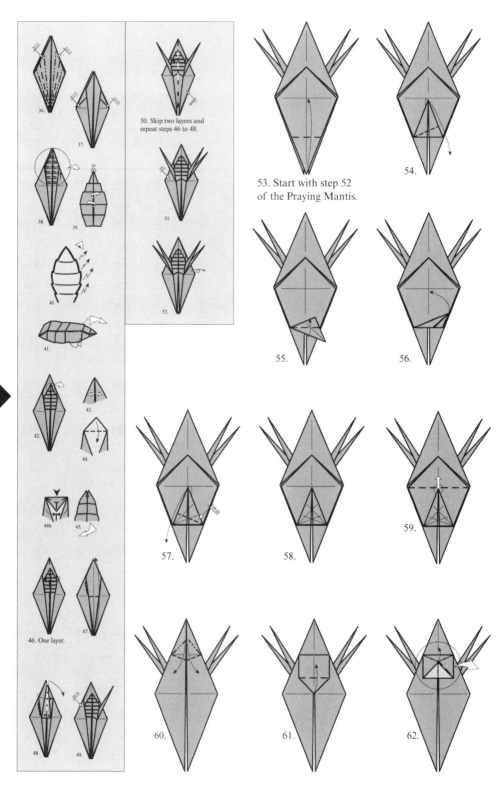

50. Skip two layers and repeat steps 46 to 48.

53. Start with step 52 of the Praying Mantis.

46. One layer.

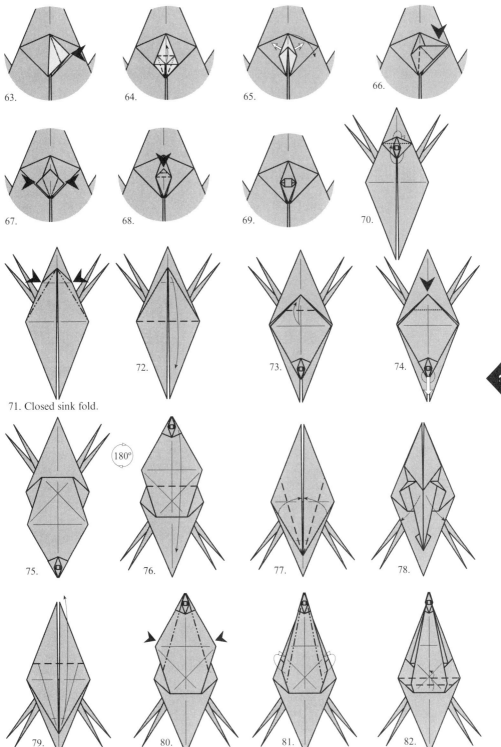

63.

64.

65.

66.

67.

68.

69.

70.

71. Closed sink fold.

72.

73.

74.

75.

180°

76.

77.

78.

79.

80.

81.

82.

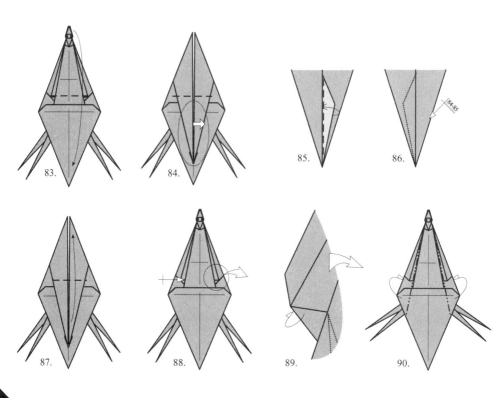

83.

84.

85.

86.

87.

88.

89.

90.

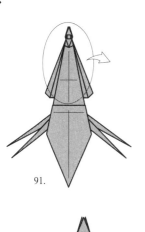

91.

92.

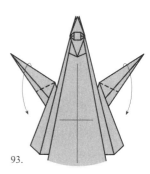

93.

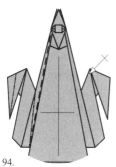

94.

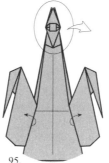

95.

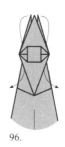

96.

97.

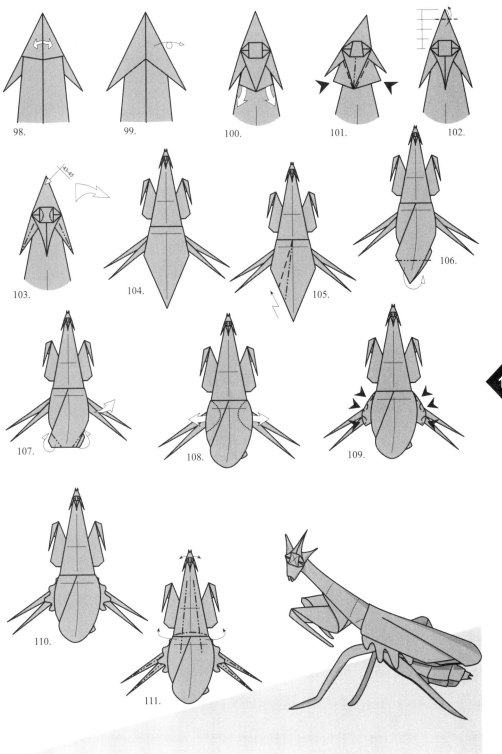

98.

99.

100.

101.

102.

103.

104.

105.

106.

107.

108.

109.

121

110.

111.

Wasp

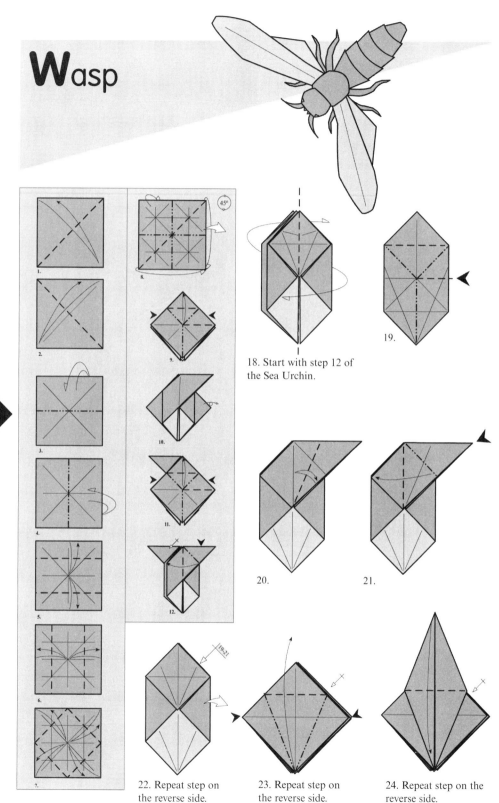

18. Start with step 12 of the Sea Urchin.

19.

20.

21.

22. Repeat step on the reverse side.

23. Repeat step on the reverse side.

24. Repeat step on the reverse side.

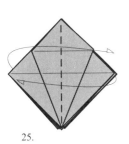

25.

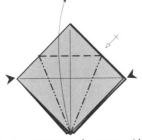

26. Repeat step on the reverse side.

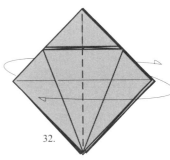

27. Repeat step on the reverse side.

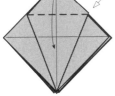

28. Repeat step on the reverse side.

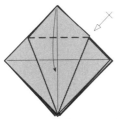

29. Repeat step on the reverse side.

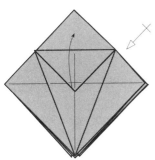

30. Repeat step on the reverse side.

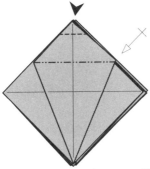

31. Repeat step on the reverse side.

32.

123

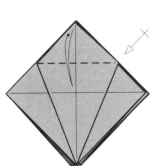

33. Repeat step on the reverse side.

34. Stretch.

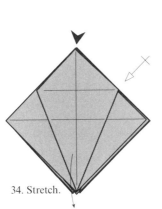

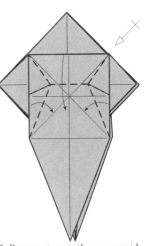

35. Repeat step on the reverse side.

36.

37.

38.

39.

40.

124

41.

42.

43.

44. Repeat.

45. Fold both tips toward the right.

46.

47. Repeat step on the reverse side.

48.

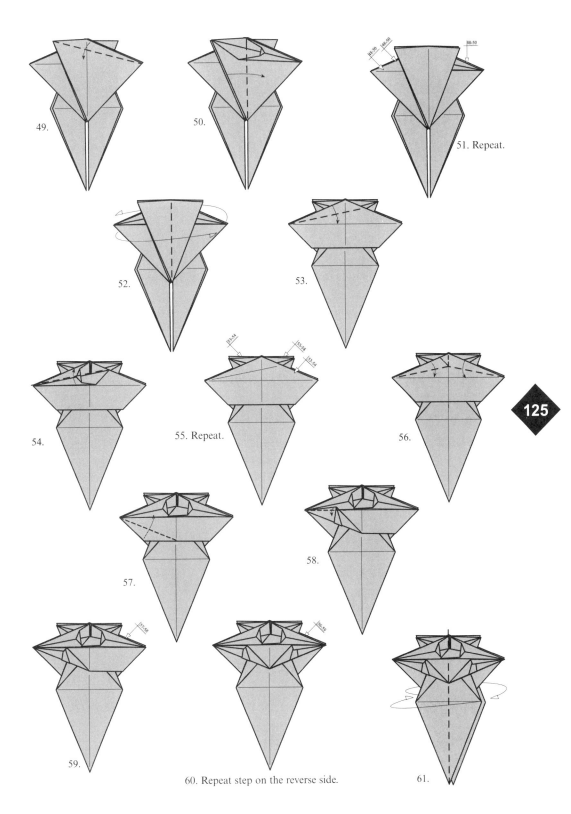

49.

50.

51. Repeat.

52.

53.

54.

55. Repeat.

56.

57.

58.

59.

60. Repeat step on the reverse side.

61.

125

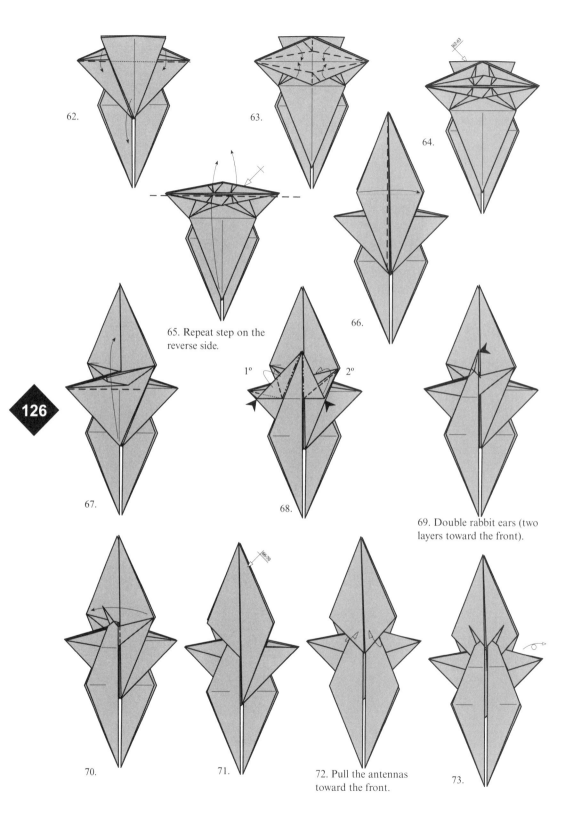

62.

63.

64.

65. Repeat step on the reverse side.

66.

126

67.

1° 2°

68.

69. Double rabbit ears (two layers toward the front).

70.

71.

72. Pull the antennas toward the front.

73.

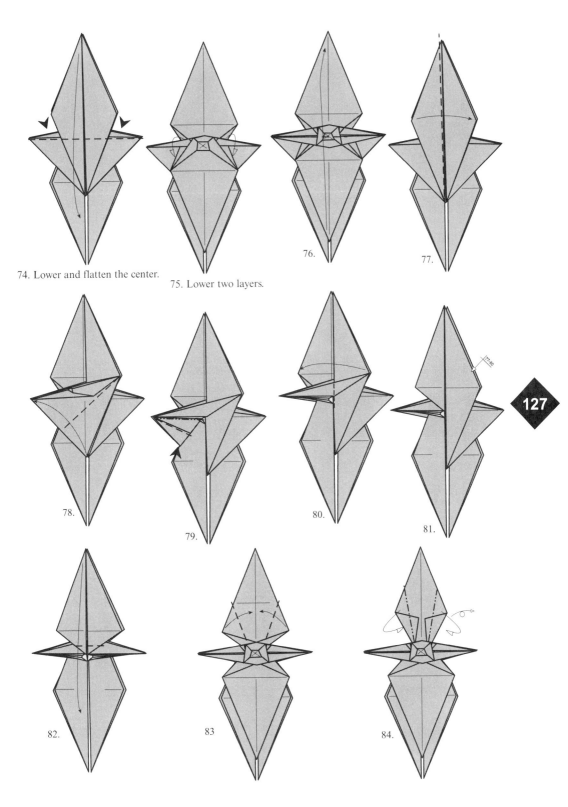

74. Lower and flatten the center.

75. Lower two layers.

76.

77.

78.

79.

80.

81.

82.

83.

84.

127

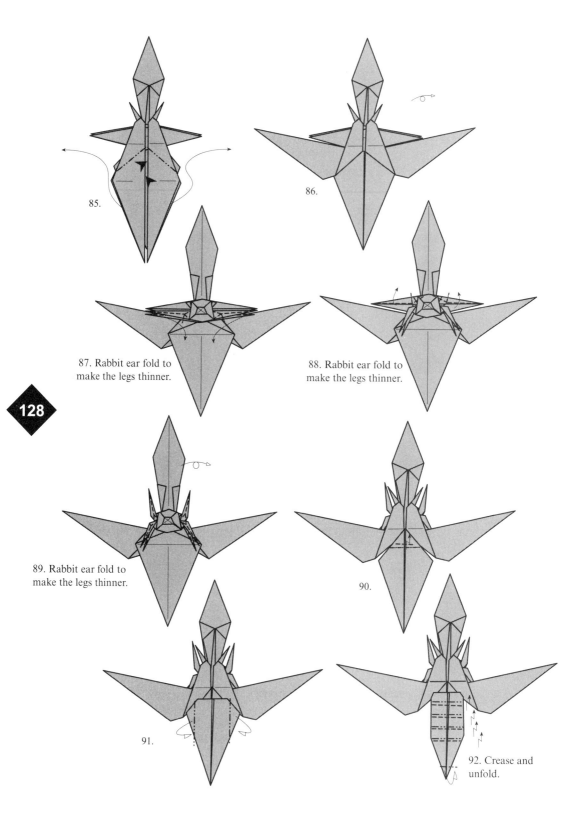

85.

86.

87. Rabbit ear fold to make the legs thinner.

88. Rabbit ear fold to make the legs thinner.

89. Rabbit ear fold to make the legs thinner.

90.

91.

92. Crease and unfold.

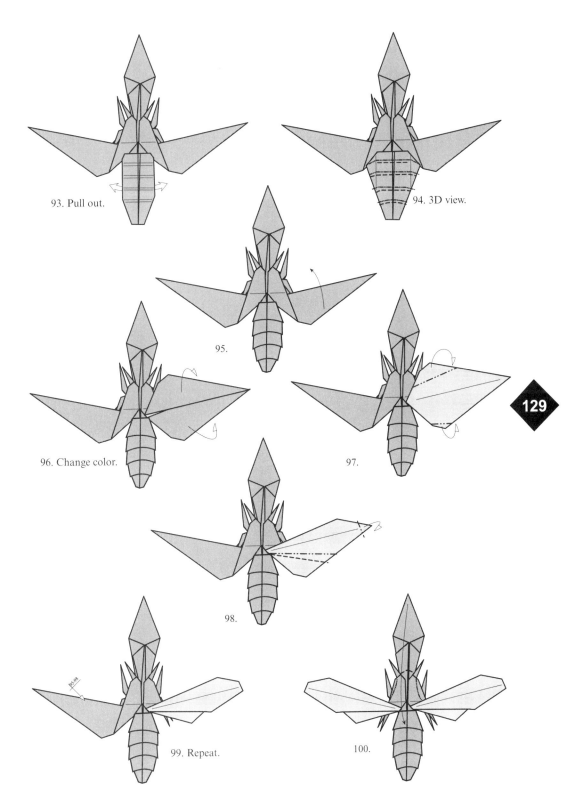

93. Pull out.

94. 3D view.

95.

96. Change color.

97.

98.

99. Repeat.

100.

129

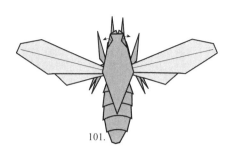

101.

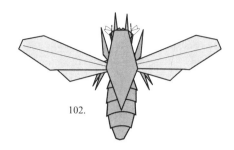

102.

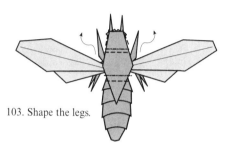

103. Shape the legs.

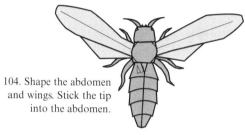

104. Shape the abdomen and wings. Stick the tip into the abdomen.

Butterfly

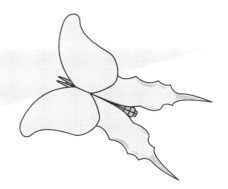

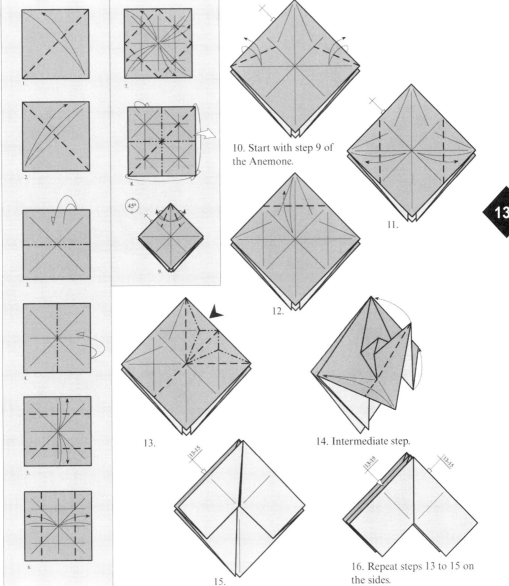

10. Start with step 9 of the Anemone.

11.

12.

13.

14. Intermediate step.

15.

16. Repeat steps 13 to 15 on the sides.

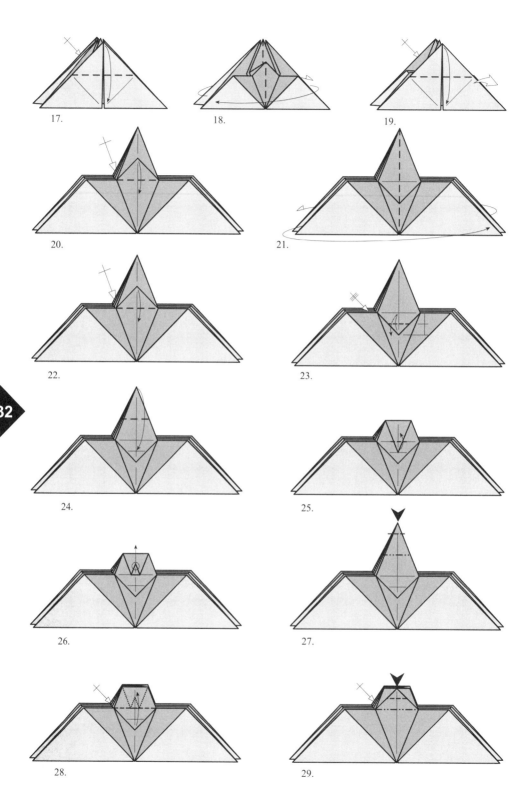

17.

18.

19.

20.

21.

22.

23.

132

24.

25.

26.

27.

28.

29.

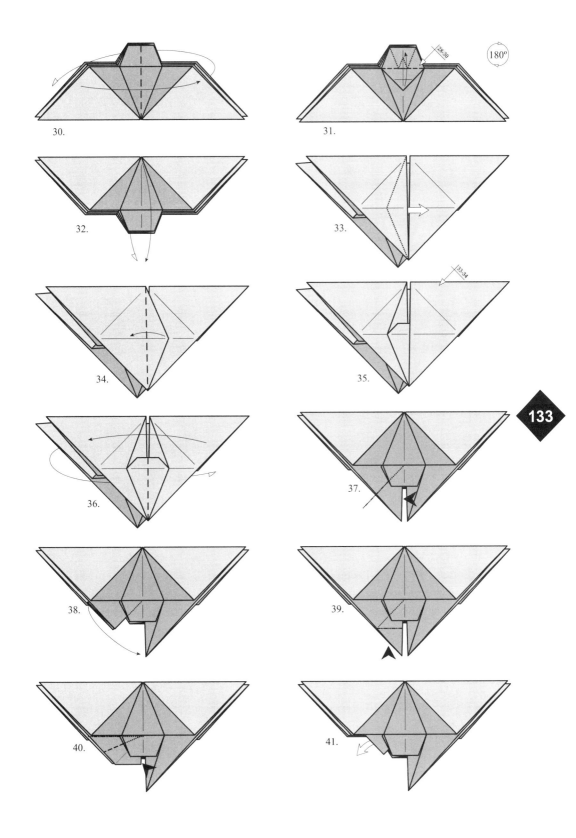

30.

31.

180°

32.

33.

34.

35.

133

37.

36.

38.

39.

40.

41.

42.

43.

44.

45.

46. Move the head upwards.

47.

48.

49.

50.

51.

52.

53.

54.

55-A.

55-B. Move the abdomen upwards while you fold it toward the reverse side.

56.

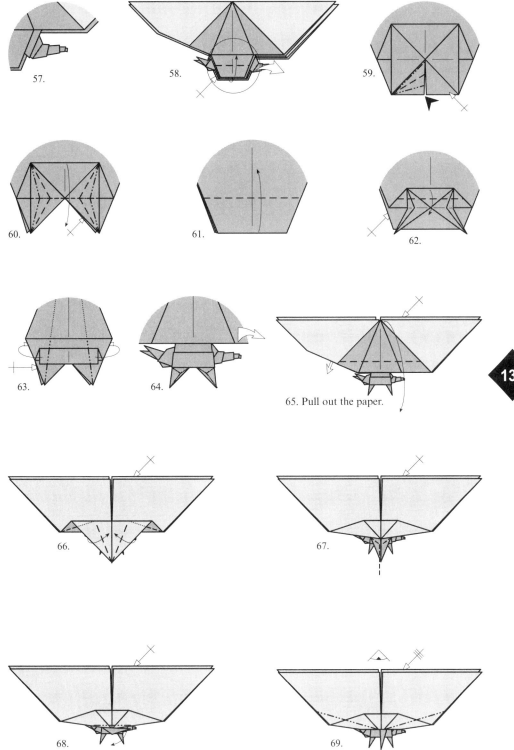

57.

58.

59.

60.

61.

62.

63.

64.

65. Pull out the paper.

135

66.

67.

68.

69.

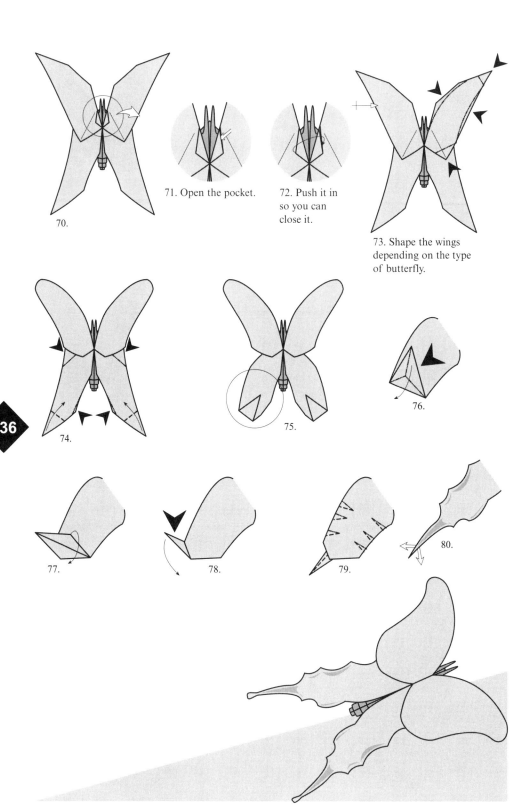

70.

71. Open the pocket.

72. Push it in so you can close it.

73. Shape the wings depending on the type of butterfly.

74.

75.

76.

77.

78.

79.

80.

part

4

Orb-weaver Spider

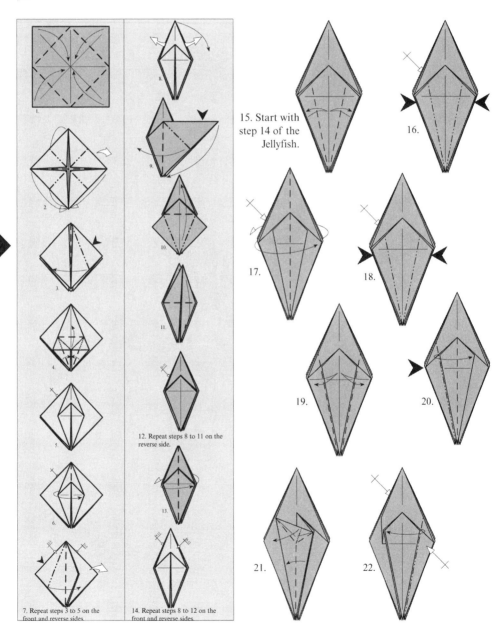

1.

2.

3.

4.

5.

6.

7. Repeat steps 3 to 5 on the front and reverse sides.

8.

9.

10.

11.

12. Repeat steps 8 to 11 on the reverse side.

13.

14. Repeat steps 8 to 12 on the front and reverse sides.

15. Start with step 14 of the Jellyfish.

16.

17.

18.

19.

20.

21.

22.

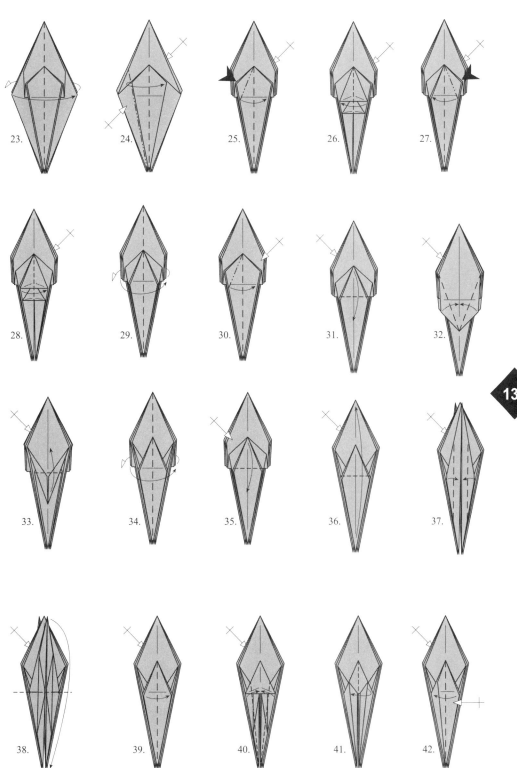

23.

24.

25.

26.

27.

28.

29.

30.

31.

32.

139

33.

34.

35.

36.

37.

38.

39.

40.

41.

42.

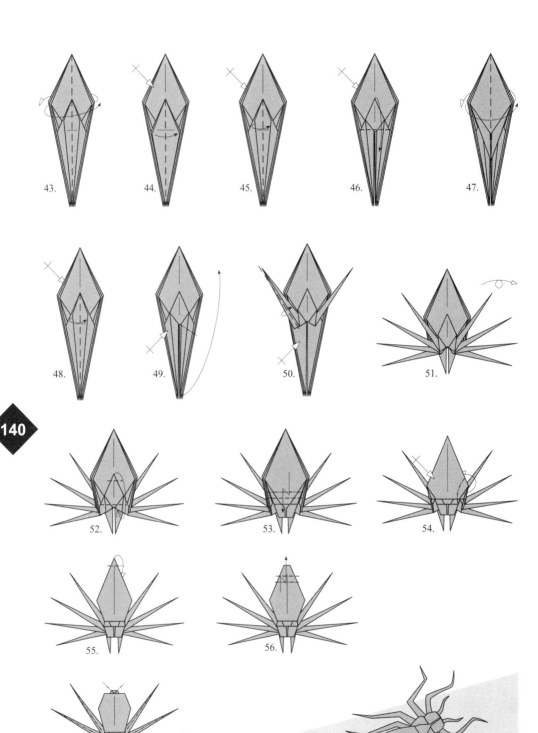

43.

44.

45.

46.

47.

48.

49.

50.

51.

52.

53.

54.

55.

56.

57.

Red-legged Spider

1.
2.
3.
4.
5.
6.
7.
8.
9.
10.
11.
12.

13. Repeat steps 6 to 12.

14. Start with step 14 of the Jellyfish.

15.

16.
17.
18.
19.
20.
21.

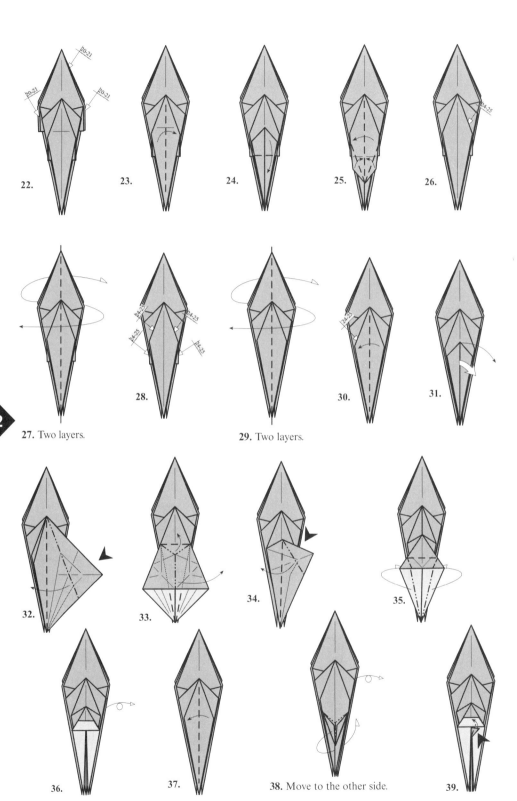

142

22.

23.

24.

25.

26.

27. Two layers.

28.

29. Two layers.

30.

31.

32.

33.

34.

35.

36.

37.

38. Move to the other side.

39.

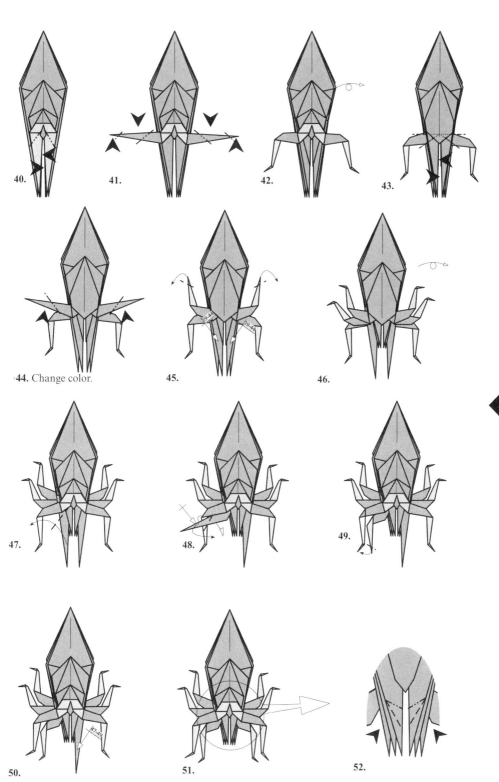

40.

41.

42.

43.

44. Change color.

45.

46.

47.

48.

49.

50.

51.

52.

143

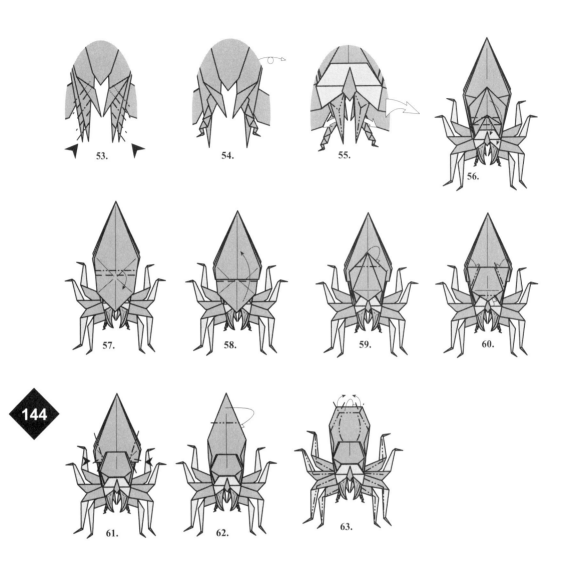

53.

54.

55.

56.

57.

58.

59.

60.

61.

62.

63.

Tarantula

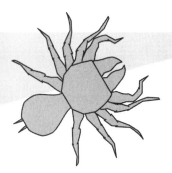

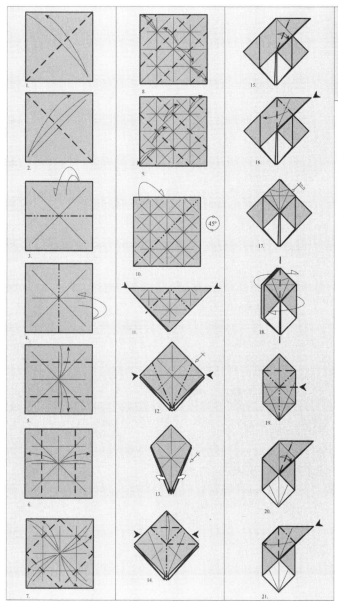

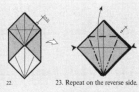

23. Repeat on the reverse side.

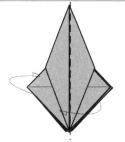

24. Start with step 23 of the Wasp.

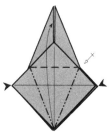

25. Repeat on the reverse side.

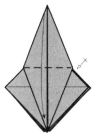

26. Repeat on the reverse side.

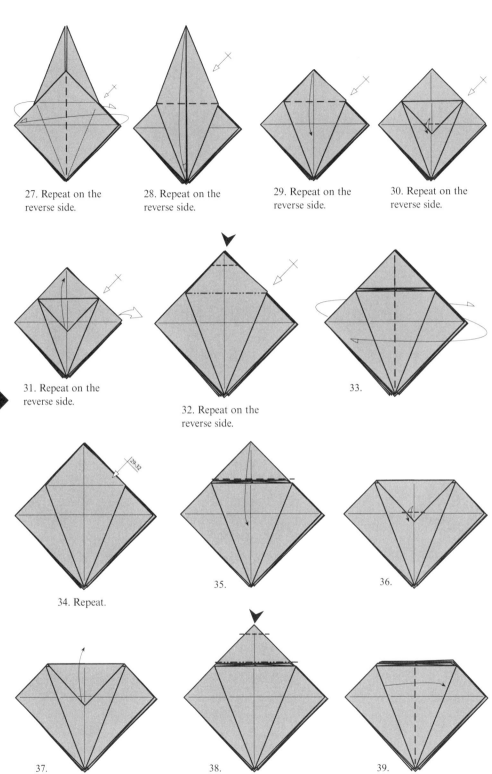

27. Repeat on the reverse side.

28. Repeat on the reverse side.

29. Repeat on the reverse side.

30. Repeat on the reverse side.

31. Repeat on the reverse side.

32. Repeat on the reverse side.

33.

34. Repeat.

35.

36.

37.

38.

39.

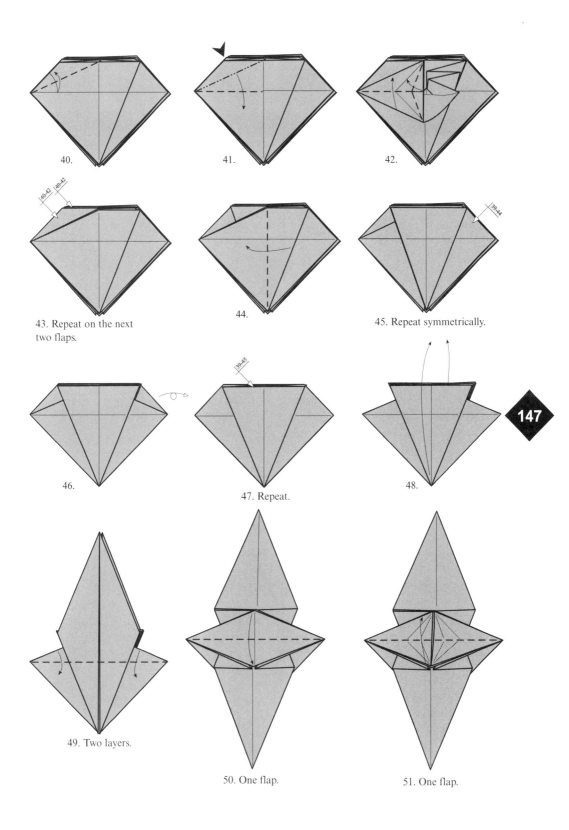

40.

41.

42.

43. Repeat on the next
two flaps.

44.

45. Repeat symmetrically.

46.

47. Repeat.

48.

147

49. Two layers.

50. One flap.

51. One flap.

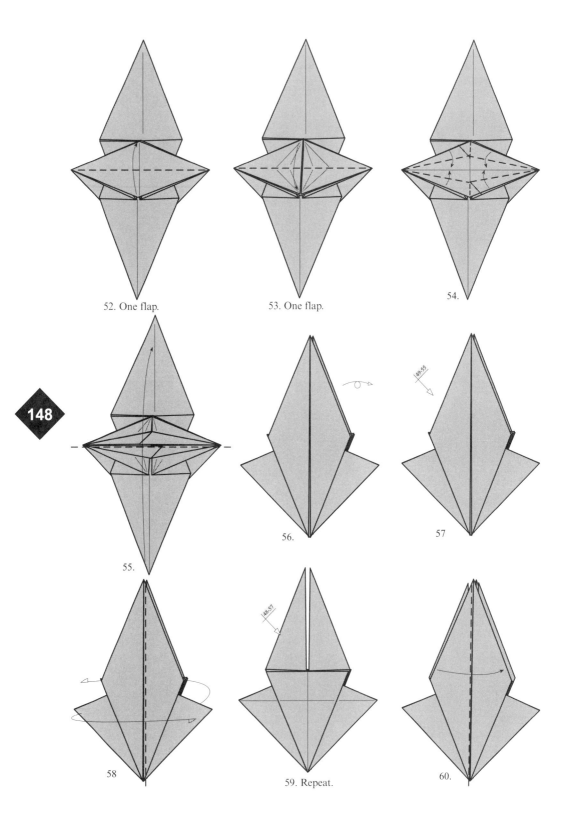

52. One flap.

53. One flap.

54.

55.

56.

57

58

59. Repeat.

60.

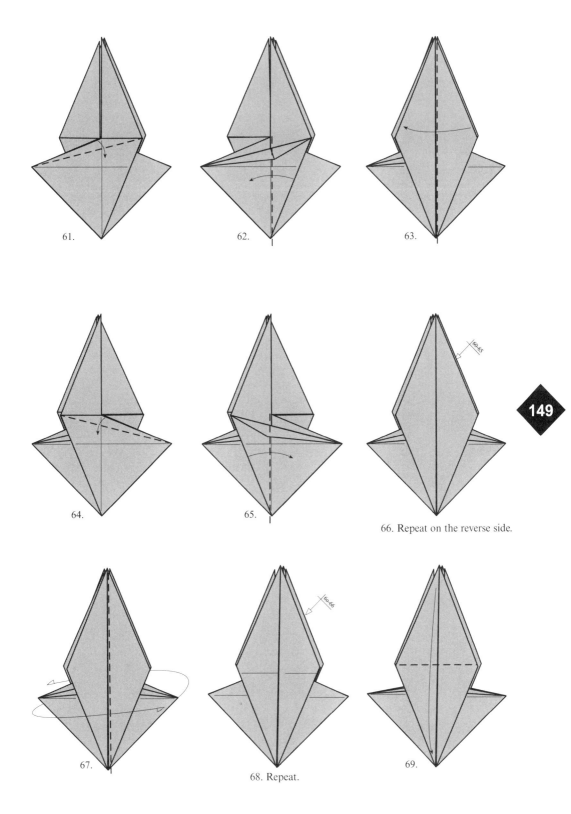

61.

62.

63.

64.

65.

66. Repeat on the reverse side.

67.

68. Repeat.

69.

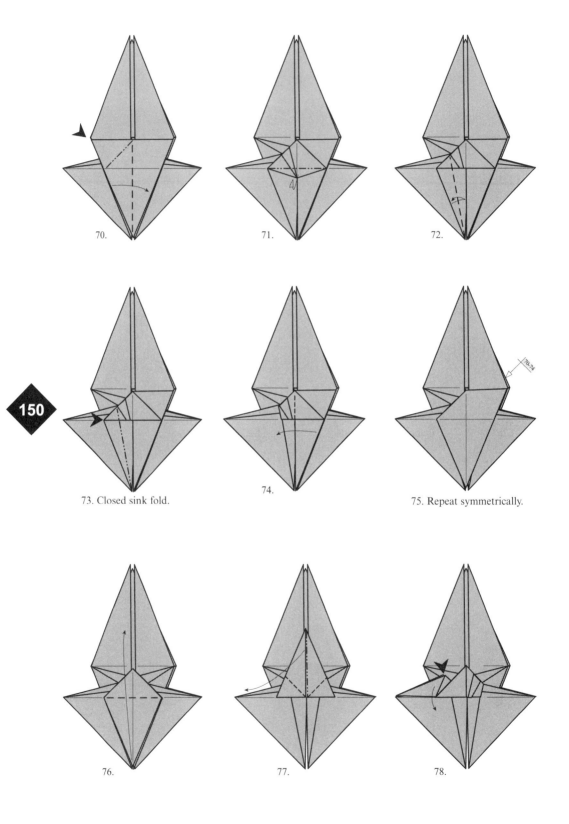

70.

71.

72.

150

73. Closed sink fold.

74.

75. Repeat symmetrically.

76.

77.

78.

79.

80.

81.

82. Repeat.

83.

84. 3D step.

85. 3D step.

86. Repeat on the reverse side.

87.

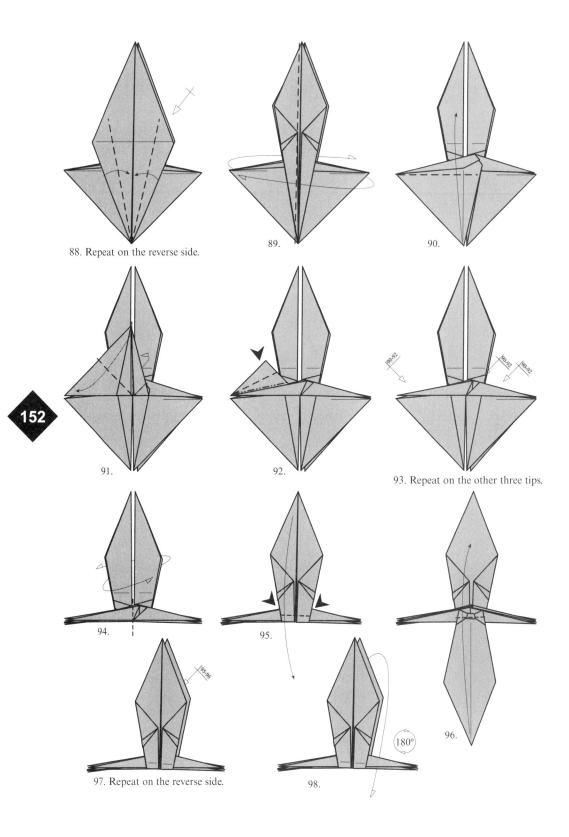

88. Repeat on the reverse side.

89.

90.

152

91.

92.

93. Repeat on the other three tips.

94.

95.

96.

97. Repeat on the reverse side.

98.

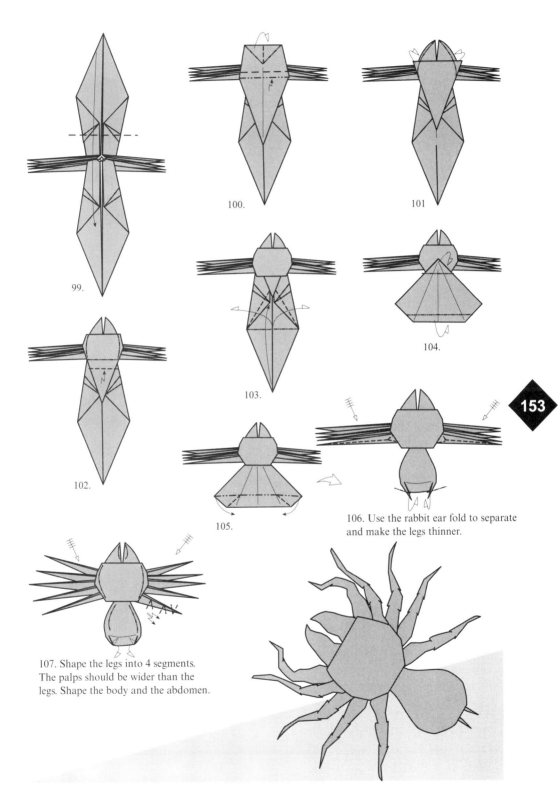

99.

100.

101

102.

103.

104.

105.

106. Use the rabbit ear fold to separate and make the legs thinner.

107. Shape the legs into 4 segments. The palps should be wider than the legs. Shape the body and the abdomen.

153

Scorpion

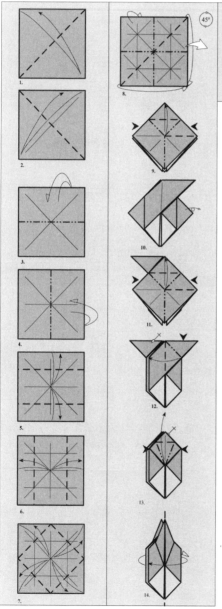

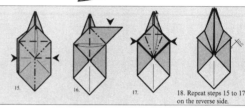

15. 16. 17. 18. Repeat steps 15 to 17 on the reverse side.

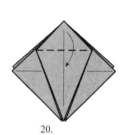

19. Start with step 18 of the Harlequin Beetle.

20.

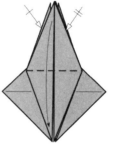

21.

22.

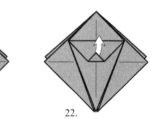

23.

24.

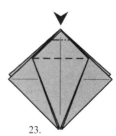

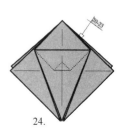

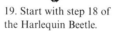

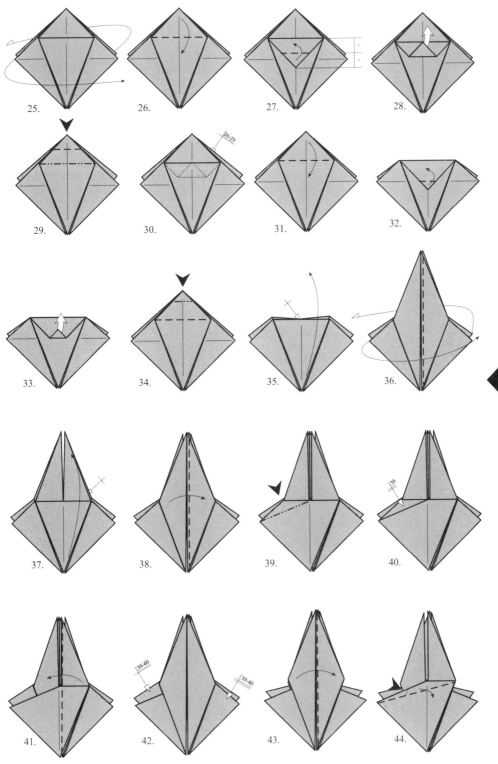

25.

26.

27.

28.

29.

30.

31.

32.

33.

34.

35.

36.

37.

38.

39.

40.

41.

42.

43.

44.

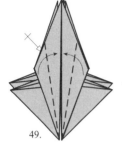

45.

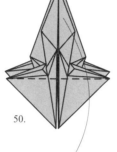

46.

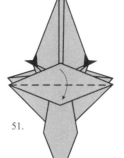

47.

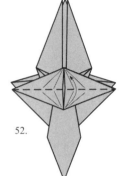

48.

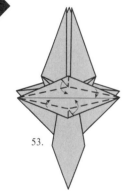

49.

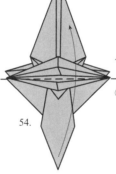

50.

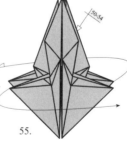

51.

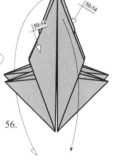

52.

53.

54.

55.

56.

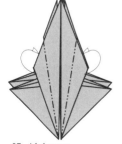

57. Abdomen

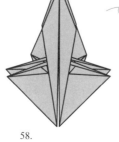

58.

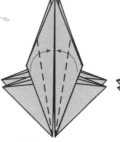

59. Thorax

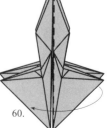

60.

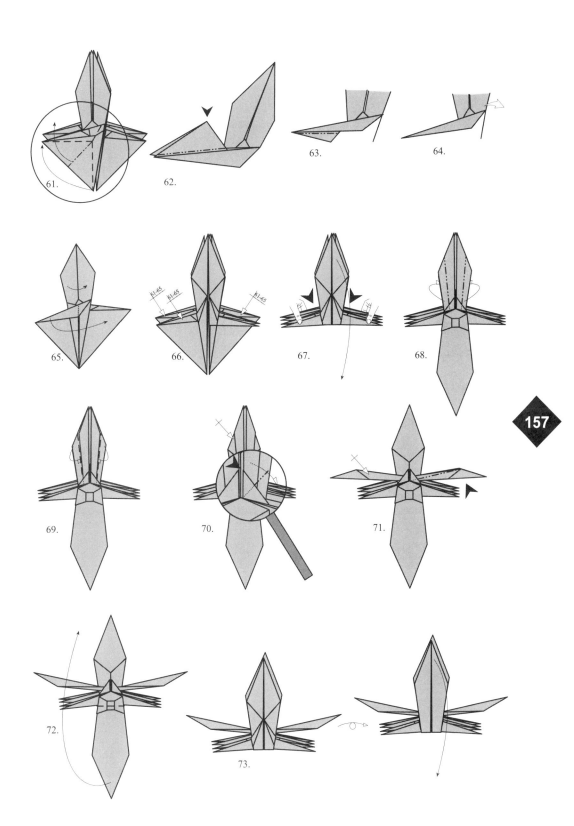

61.

62.

63.

64.

65.

66.

67.

68.

69.

70.

71.

72.

73.

74.

75. Two tips.

76.

158

77.

78.

79. Two tips.

80.

81.

82. Use the
rabbit ear fold
on each leg.

83.

84. 7 rings

85.

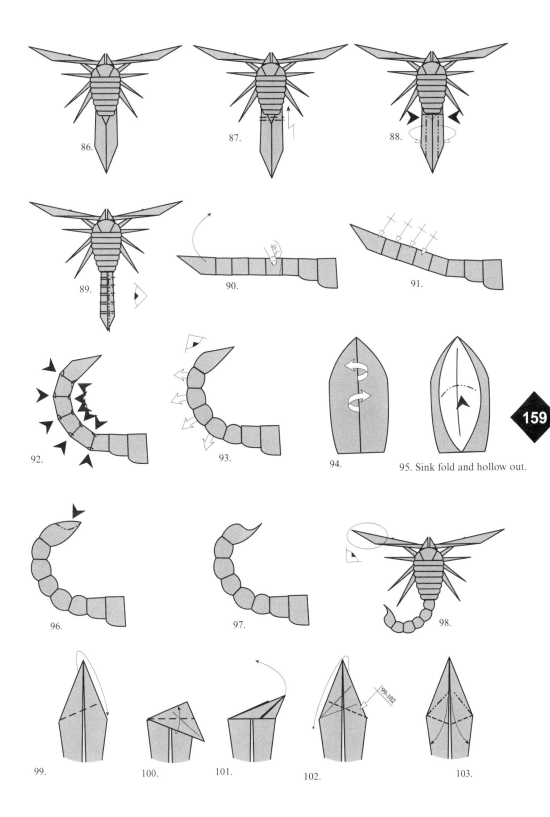

86.

87.

88.

89.

90.

91.

92.

93.

94.

95. Sink fold and hollow out.

159

96.

97.

98.

99.

100.

101.

102.

99-102

103.

 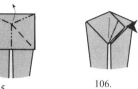

  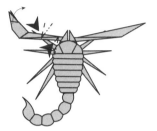

104.   105.   106.   107.   108.

109.   110.

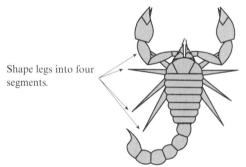

111.

160

112. Pull out the paper and shape into a round form.

Shape legs into four segments.

part

161

Europen Tree Frog

1.

2.

3.

4.

5.

6.

7.

8.

9.

10.

11.

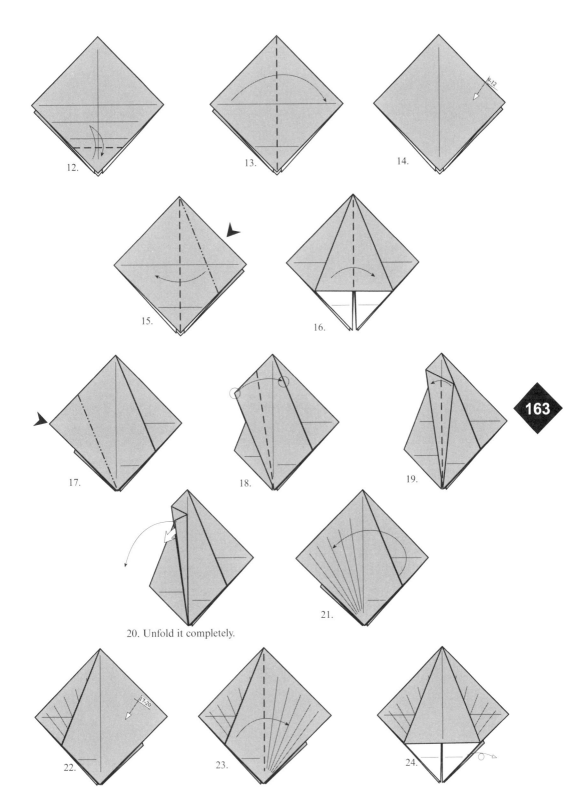

12.

13.

14.

15.

16.

17.

18.

19.

20. Unfold it completely.

21.

22.

23.

24.

25.

26.

27.

28.

29.

30.

31.

32.

33. Open.

34.

35.

36.

37.

38.

39.

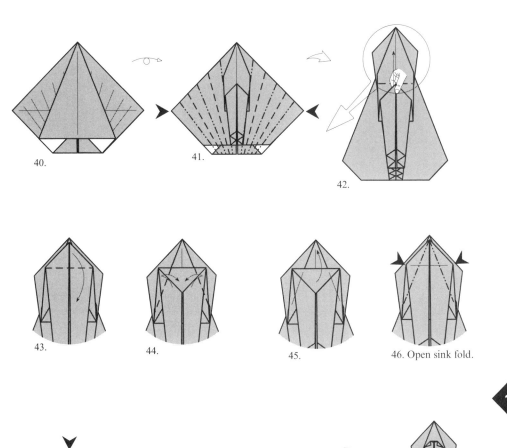

40.

41.

42.

43.

44.

45.

46. Open sink fold.

47. Open.

48.

49.

50.

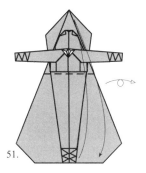

51.

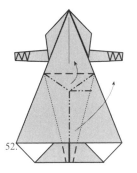

52.

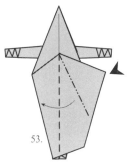

53.

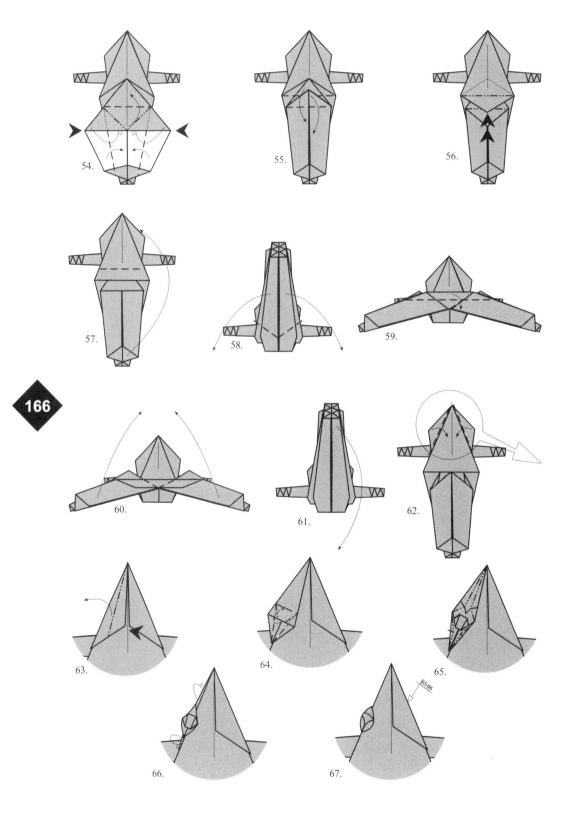

54.

55.

56.

57.

58.

59.

60.

61.

62.

63.

64.

65.

66.

67.

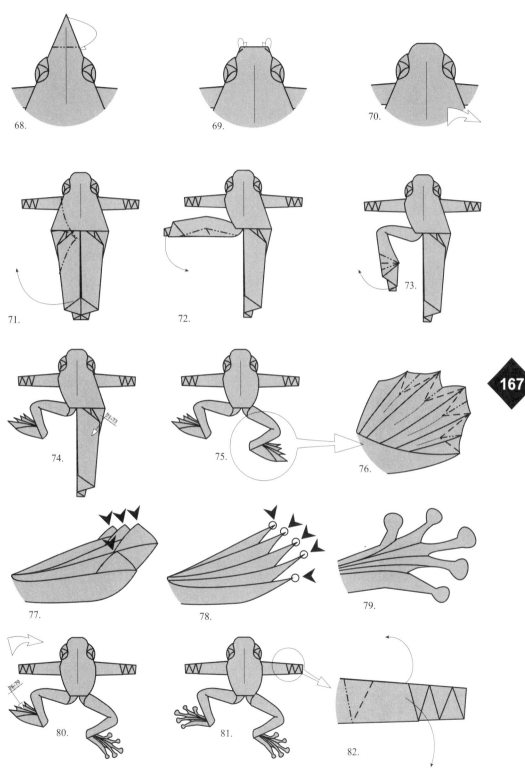

68.

69.

70.

71.

72.

73.

74.

75.

76.

77.

78.

79.

80.

81.

82.

83.

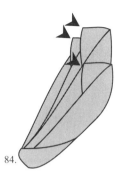

84.

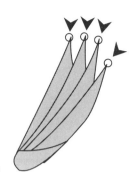

85.

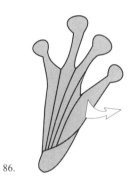

86.

83-86

Centaurea

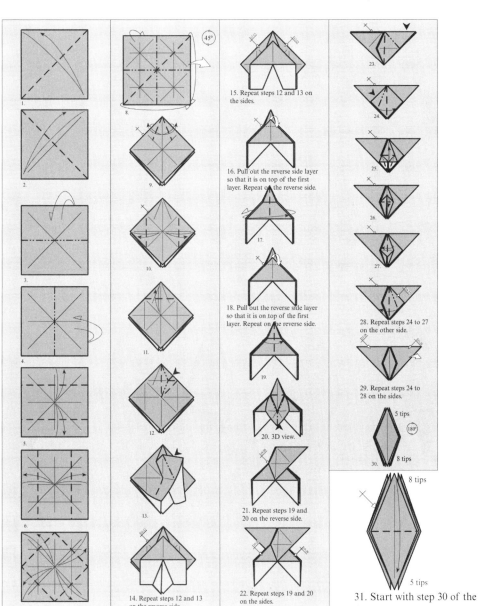

15. Repeat steps 12 and 13 on the sides.

16. Pull out the reverse side layer so that it is on top of the first layer. Repeat on the reverse side.

18. Pull out the reverse side layer so that it is on top of the first layer. Repeat on the reverse side.

20. 3D view.

21. Repeat steps 19 and 20 on the reverse side.

22. Repeat steps 19 and 20 on the sides.

14. Repeat steps 12 and 13 on the reverse side.

28. Repeat steps 24 to 27 on the other side.

29. Repeat steps 24 to 28 on the sides.

5 tips

8 tips

8 tips

5 tips

31. Start with step 30 of the Anemone.

169

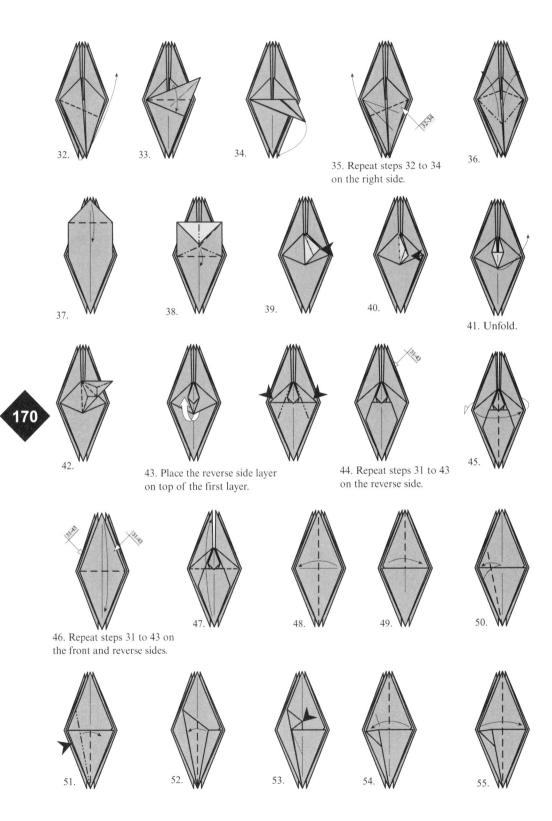

32.

33.

34.

35. Repeat steps 32 to 34 on the right side.

36.

37.

38.

39.

40.

41. Unfold.

170

42.

43. Place the reverse side layer on top of the first layer.

44. Repeat steps 31 to 43 on the reverse side.

45.

46. Repeat steps 31 to 43 on the front and reverse sides.

47.

48.

49.

50.

51.

52.

53.

54.

55.

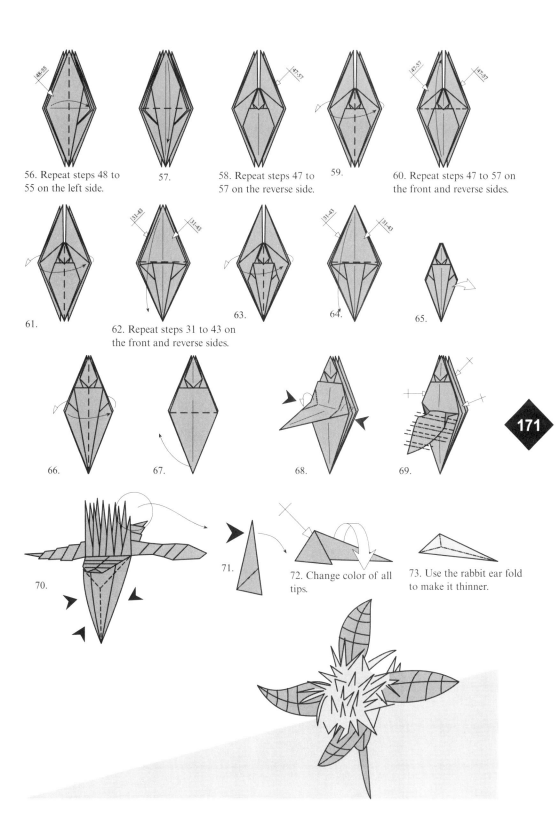

56. Repeat steps 48 to 55 on the left side.

57.

58. Repeat steps 47 to 57 on the reverse side.

59.

60. Repeat steps 47 to 57 on the front and reverse sides.

61.

62. Repeat steps 31 to 43 on the front and reverse sides.

63.

64.

65.

66.

67.

68.

69.

171

70.

71.

72. Change color of all tips.

73. Use the rabbit ear fold to make it thinner.

Leatherback Sea Turtle

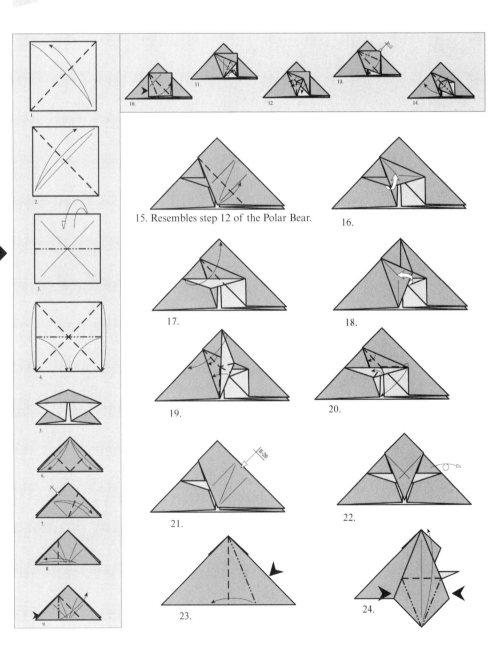

15. Resembles step 12 of the Polar Bear.

16.

17.

18.

19.

20.

21.

22.

23.

24.

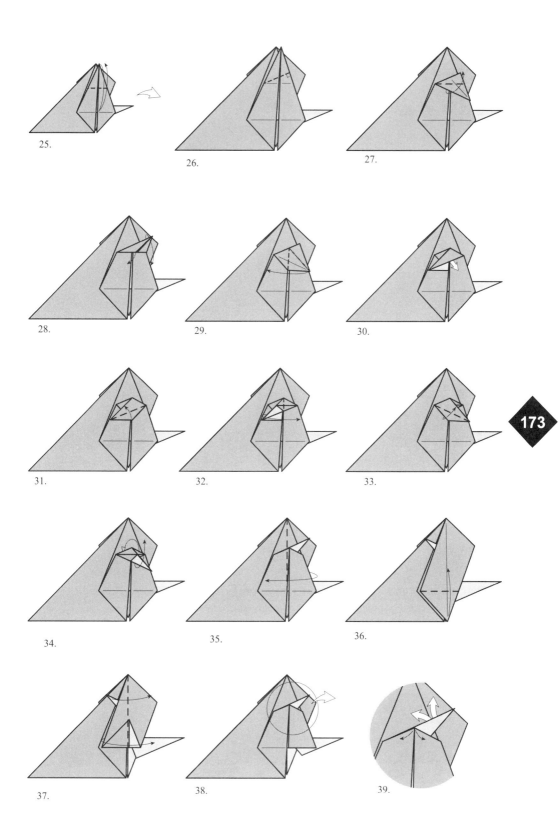

25.

26.

27.

28.

29.

30.

31.

32.

33.

173

34.

35.

36.

37.

38.

39.

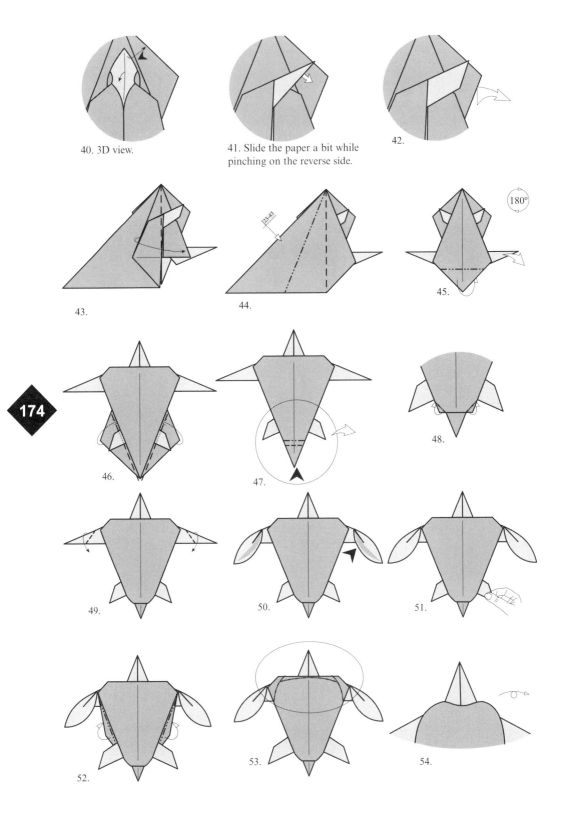

40. 3D view.

41. Slide the paper a bit while pinching on the reverse side.

42.

43.

44.

45.

180°

174

46.

47.

48.

49.

50.

51.

52.

53.

54.

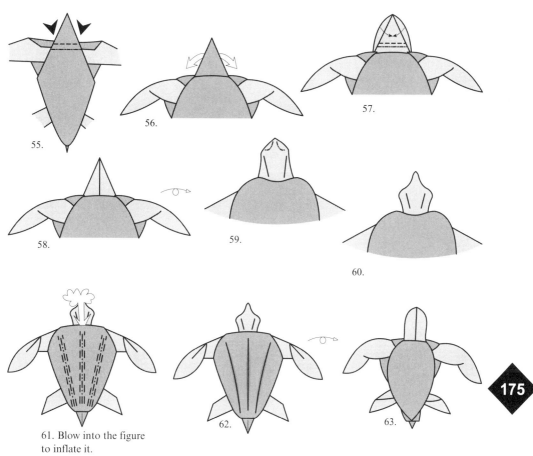

55.

56.

57.

58.

59.

60.

61. Blow into the figure to inflate it.

62.

63.

175